Ireland's Combined Second and Third Reports

under the

UN Convention on the Elimination of All Forms of Discrimination Against Women

February, 1997

BAILE ÁTHA CLIATH
ARNA FHOILSIÚ AG OIFIG AN tSOLÁTHAIR
Le ceannach díreach ón
OIFIG DHÍOLTA FOILSEACHÁN RIALTAIS,
TEACH SUN ALLIANCE, SRÁID THEACH LAIGHEAN, BAILE ÁTHA CLIATH 2,
nó tríd an bpost ó
FOILSEACHÁIN RIALTAIS, AN RANNÓG POST-TRÁCHTA,
4 - 5 BÓTHAR FHEARCHAIR, BAILE ÁTHA CLIATH 2,
(Teil: 01 - 6613111 — fo-líne 4040/4045; Fax: 01 - 4752760)
nó trí aon díoltóir leabhar.

DUBLIN
PUBLISHED BY THE STATIONERY OFFICE
To be purchased directly from the
GOVERNMENT PUBLICATIONS SALE OFFICE,
SUN ALLIANCE HOUSE, MOLESWORTH STREET, DUBLIN 2,
or by mail order from
GOVERNMENT PUBLICATIONS, POSTAL TRADE SECTION,
4 - 5 HARCOURT ROAD, DUBLIN 2,
(Tel: 01 - 6613111 — ext. 4040/4045; Fax: 01 - 4752760)
or through any bookseller.

Price: £7.00

(Pn. 3771)

ISBN 0 7076 3845 3

FOREWORD

I am pleased to introduce Ireland's combined Second and Third periodic reports under the United Nations Convention on the Elimination of All Forms of Discrimination Against Women, which were submitted to the UN on 24 March, 1997.

Ireland acceded to the Convention on 22 December, 1985 and submitted its first periodic report in February, 1987. This document highlights the considerable progress made in the intervening years.

An important milestone was the establishment of the Department of Equality and Law Reform headed by a Minister of Cabinet rank with responsibility for ensuring that equality becomes a reality through institutional, administrative and legal reforms. I was very happy to accept the trust placed in me as Minister for Equality and Law Reform and to oversee a number of very important developments since then. These are documented in this report.

Other Government Departments and bodies are also actively engaged in promoting equality, as is evident throughout this report.

Another important milestone was the publication of the report of the Second Commission on the Status of Women in January, 1993. The Commission made over 200 recommendations aimed at achieving de facto equality for Irish women. Two reports charting progress in implementing the Commission's recommendations have been published.

Ireland actively participated in the United Nations Fourth World Conference on Women and in the preparatory process. Ireland accepted the Platform for Action agreed at the Conference without reservations.

A report on progress made in implementing the Platform for Action was published in December, 1996. The report provides an overview of what is happening in Ireland and it is apparent from the report that the objectives and actions agreed at Beijing are being assimilated into all areas of Government policy in a manner appropriate to Irish conditions. Ireland is also actively involved in follow-up to the Conference at the international level.

There is, however, no room for complacency, and much work remains to be done in achieving full equality of opportunity for Irish women and men into the future. My Department will continue to play a lead role in that important and fundamental task of Government.

Mervyn Taylor TD
Minister for Equality and Law Reform

Contents

Part 1

1. General Economic and Social Background

1.1 Demography

1.1.1 Main Features of the Population

The population of Ireland enumerated on Census night 1991 was 3,525,719 persons, which represents a decrease of 0.4% on the 1986 Census count. This is the first decline in population observed since the 1961 Census. The number of females enumerated in 1991 exceeded the number of males by 18,883, continuing a pattern which re-emerged in the 1986 Census.

There was considerable variation between different age groups in the rate of population change between 1986 and 1991. This reflects not only the natural progression of the population age structure, but also the impact of births, deaths and migration.

Table A

Population of Ireland by Age Group and Sex, 1986 and 1991

Age Group	1986		1991	
	Male	Female	Male	Female
0 – 14	525,646	499,055	482,838	457,736
15 – 24	313,999	303,525	307,887	293,711
25 – 44	465,656	456,963	476,408	482,556
45 – 64	295,658	295,786	312,560	309,123
65 and over	168,631	215,624	173,725	229,175
Total	**1,769,690**	**1,770,953**	**1,753,418**	**1,772,301**

Source: Census of Population, 1986, 1991

The average number of persons per private household decreased from 3.54 in 1986 to 3.34 in 1991. The number of private households increased by 5.4 per cent between 1986 and 1991, the largest increase being 14.8 per cent for one-person households. Of these, 58 per cent were households formed by women. Private households of six persons or more declined by 14.7 per cent.

Persons aged 65 years and over accounted for 11.4 per cent of the population in 1991 compared to 10.9 per cent in 1986. A growing proportion of persons over 65 years lived alone in private households in 1991. In absolute and relative terms more females than males over 65 years lived alone in 1991.

The "young" dependency ratio (i.e. the ratio of the population aged 0-14 years to that aged 15-64 years) was 0.431 in 1991 compared to 0.481 in 1986. The "old" dependency ratio (i.e. the ratio of the population aged 65 years and over to that aged 15-64 years) increased very slightly from 0.180 in 1986 to 0.185 in 1991. Overall the total dependency ratio fell from 0.661 in 1986 to 0.616 in 1991.

Preliminary results from the 1996 Census indicates an increase of 2.7% in the population (to 3,621,035 persons). The number of females enumerated in 1996 exceeded the number of males by 25,843 continuing the pattern observed in 1986 and 1991.

1.1.2 Marital Status

The 1991 Census results show that 39.18 per cent of persons aged 15 years and over were single, 51.43 per cent were married (including remarried), 2.13 per cent were separated and 7.26 per cent were widowed. The number of single persons aged 15 years and over increased by 2.5 per cent between 1986 and 1991 while the increase was 1.9 per cent for married persons. The increase in the number of widowed persons was less than one per cent but the increase observed in the separated category was close to 50 per cent.

Table B provides a breakdown of the separated population by category and sex in 1986 and 1991. Most of the increase in the number of separated persons between 1986 and 1991 was in the "deserted" and "legally separated" categories. Over a third of separated persons were aged 35-44 years while a further quarter were in the age group 45-54 years. There were 21,350 separated males and 33,793 separated females equivalent to 3.1 per cent and 4.8 per cent respectively, of the corresponding total of ever-married, excluding widowed persons. These rates varied between age groups and counties.

Table B

Separated Persons Classified by Category and Sex, 1986 and 1991

SEPARATED	MALE				FEMALE			
	1986	1986 %	1991	1991 %	1986	1986 %	1991	1991 %
Deserted	2,584	17.65	6,781	31.77	9,038	39.98	16,904	50.02
Marriage annulled	443	3.03	499	2.34	540	2.39	722	2.14
Legally separated	3,299	22.54	5,178	24.25	3,888	17.20	5,974	17.68
Other separated	6,090	41.60	5,787	27.10	6,972	30.84	7,195	21.29
Divorced in another country	2,222	15.18	3,105	14.54	2,169	9.59	2,998	8.87
Total	**14,638**	**100.00**	**21,350**	**100.00**	**22,607**	**100.00**	**33,793**	**100.00**

Source: Census of Population, 1991

1.1.3 Births, Marriages and Deaths

Total births declined from a peak of 74,064 in 1980 to 48,530 in 1995. The annual birth rate per 1,000 population declined from 22.7 in 1971 to 13.5 in 1995. The declining birth rate has been accompanied by an increase in the number of births outside marriage – from 10.9% in 1987 to 22.2% in 1995. The total fertility rate (i.e. the average number of children expected to be born to a woman over her child-bearing years) fell to 1.87 in 1995, which is below the replacement level.

The average age of women at first marriage reached a low point of 24 in 1979 and since then has steadily increased to 26.3 in 1990, reflecting wider social change. The marriage rate has also declined; see Table C. The decline in the proportion of women who are married is especially marked for those in the younger age groups.

Infant mortality rates (under 1 year) declined from 19.5 per 1,000 live births in 1970 to 6.3 in 1995.

Maternal deaths per 1,000 live and still births were 0.02 in 1994, with none in 1993.

Table C

Marriages, Births and Deaths and Rates per 1,000 of the Population

DESCRIPTIONS	1987	1988	1989	1990	1991	1992	1993	1994	1995
Marriages	**18,309**	**18,382**	**18,174**	**17,838**	**16,859**	**16,109**	**15,728**	**16,297**	**15,623**
BIRTHS:									
Male	29,931	28,083	26,754	27,559	27,143	26,567	25,449	24,744	25,032
Female	28,502	26,517	25,264	25,485	25,547	24,990	24,007	23,185	23,498
Total	**58,433**	**54,600**	**52,018**	**53,044**	**52,690**	**51,557**	**49,456**	**47,929**	**48,530**
Births within Marriage	52,086	48,117	45,347	45,277	43,924	42,258	39,792	38,479	37,742
Births outside Marriage	6,347	6,483	6,671	7,767	8,766	9,299	9,664	9,450	10,788
Births outside Marriage as % of total Births	10.9	11.9	12.8	14.6	16.6	18.0	19.5	19.7	22.2
DEATHS:									
Male	17,002	16,980	17,058	16,828	16,741	16,491	16,783	16,219	16,680
Female	14,411	14,600	15,053	14,542	14,757	14,457	14,873	14,525	14,814
Total	**31,413**	**31,580**	**32,111**	**31,370**	**31,498**	**30,948**	**31,656**	**30,744**	**31,494**
Natural Increase	27,020	23,020	19,907	21,674	21,192	20,609	17,800	17,185	17,036
RATES PER 1,000 OF ESTIMATED POPULATION:									
Marriages	5.2	5.2	5.2	5.1	4.8	4.6	4.4	4.6	4.4
Births	16.5	15.4	14.8	15.1	15	14.5	13.9	13.4	13.5
Deaths	8.9	8.9	9.1	9	8.9	8.7	8.9	8.6	8.8

Sources: Statistical Abstract and Department of Health Vital Statistics, Central Statistics Office

1.1.4 Religion

The predominant religion in Ireland is Roman Catholic. Table D shows the population classified by religion and sex.

In the course of the examination of Ireland's First Report in February, 1989 a question was raised concerning the effect of religion on family life.

Ireland has a high (but declining) level of religious observance and a denominational system of education, and the influence of the Churches on attitudes can be significant. The role of women in the Roman Catholic Church is a matter of interest and concern to an increasing number within that Church.

Submissions made to the Second Commission on the Status of Women (see 3.3) indicated that many women feel that the Churches have not realised their responsibilities towards them.

The decline in the Irish birth rate and the fall in the size of completed families indicates the extent to which couples are controlling their own fertility, despite Roman Catholic teaching which prohibits all forms of artificial contraception.

The separation between Church and State is reflected in areas where social legislation is brought forward independently of the stated position of Churches.

Table D

Population classified by Religion and Sex

Denomination	1981		1991			
	%	Persons	Persons	%	Males	Females
Roman Catholic	93.06	3,204,476	3,228,327	91.57	1,595,688	1,632,639
Church of Ireland*	2.77	95,366	82,840	2.35	40,681	42,159
Protestant	-	-	6,347	0.18	3,037	3,310
Presbyterian	0.41	14,255	13,199	0.37	6,686	6,513
Methodist	0.17	5,790	5,037	0.14	2,412	2,625
Jewish	0.06	2,127	1,581	0.04	782	799
Other stated religions	0.32	10,843	38,743	1.10	19,948	18,795
No religion	1.15	39,572	66,270	1.88	40,205	26,065
Not stated	2.06	70,976	83,375	2.37	43,979	39,396
Total	**100.00**	**3,443,405**	**3,525,719**	**100.00**	**1,753,418**	**1,772,301**

* Includes Protestant in 1981

Source: Census of Population, 1981 and 1991.

1.2 Economic and Labour Market Factors

The Irish industrial sector is characterised by duality, i.e. a largely foreign owned, export-oriented, highly productive and profitable modern sector and the more traditional labour-intensive indigenous industries which are more oriented towards the domestic and United Kingdom markets. Industrial policy is being re-orientated towards promoting linkages between the two sectors.

Certain unusual labour market characteristics responsible for the relatively high level of unemployment (a rate of 11.25% in 1996) are:

- the natural growth rate of population although now falling has been considerably higher than the EU average in recent years generating a net annual increase in the labour force of approximately 20,000;
- the participation of married women in the labour force is tending to rise towards the EU norm from a low base.

1996 was another year of exceptionally strong growth for the Irish economy with GNP expanding by an estimated 6.25%. Domestic demand was particularly strong, with volume growth in fixed investment and private consumption estimated at 10.25% and 6% respectively. The external sector also performed well in 1996 with exports of goods and services estimated to have expanded by 10.25% by comparison with 1995. Inflation fell to just 1.6% on average last year, while there was an estimated rise of 50,000 in total employment. The General Government Deficit amounted to an estimated 1% of GDP.

In 1997 GNP is expected to expand by about 5.5%. Private consumption and investment should again make major contributions to overall growth, while the recovery in many of Ireland's key trading partners should facilitate a further strong rise in exports.

Inflation is expected to remain low in 1997, while the balance of payments should continue in surplus. Government borrowing will remain low, with the General Government Deficit projected at just 1.5% of GDP in 1997, thereby facilitating a further reduction in the General Government Debt as a percentage of GDP.

Notwithstanding the negative impact of structural and demographic factors unemployment has declined in response to increases in employment. In the period April 93-96 unemployment fell by 40,000 as measured by the Labour Force Survey. In common with most other EU countries, the Labour Force Survey rather than the Live Register is considered to be the most appropriate measure of unemployment. Accordingly, it is clear that significant progress has been made in combating unemployment.

Between 1971 and 1996, the female labour force grew from 286,000 to 540,200 an increase of almost 89%. In the same period, the number of women actually at work increased from 275,500 to 488,000, an increase of almost 77%. While the female participation rate has increased from 27.9% in 1971 to over 38.5% in 1996, Irish female participation rates are low by international standards. In mid-April, 1996, almost 41% of females aged 15 and over described themselves as being on home duties. There has been a significant increase in the participation of married women. The latest available data show that, in 1996, 36.6% of all married women were in the labour force, compared with 22.9% in 1987.

The trend in participation by married women is upwards. In 1996 the highest participation rates for married women were in the 20-24 and 25-34 age groups. The participation rate for married women aged 20-24 was 52.4% and 57.9% for women aged 25-34. By contrast, the participation rate for married women aged 35-45 was 45.9% while the rate for married women aged 45-54 was lower, at 33.3%.

2. Political and Legal Framework

2.1 The Constitution of Ireland

The basic law of the State is the Constitution of Ireland adopted in 1937. The Constitution states that all legislative, executive and judicial powers of Government derive from the people. It sets out the form of Government and defines the powers of the President, the Oireachtas (Parliament) and the Government. It also defines the structure and powers of the Courts, sets out fundamental rights of citizens and contains a number of directive principles of social policy for the general guidance of the Oireachtas. Citizens' rights cover five broad headings: personal rights, the family, education, private property and religion. The Constitution can only be amended by referendum and legislation which conflicts with the Constitution is invalid to the extent of such inconsistency.

A Constitution Review Group was established by the Government in April 1995, to review the Constitution and establish areas where constitutional change may be necessary. The report of the Review Group was published by the Government on 3 July, 1996 and is now being considered by the Oireachtas All Party Committee on the Constitution.

2.2 Government

Ireland is a sovereign, independent, parliamentary democracy. The Oireachtas consists of the President and two Houses: a House of Representatives (Dáil Éireann) and a Senate (Seanad Éireann).

Under the Constitution, the sole power of making laws is vested in the Oireachtas. The only exception is in the area of European Union law where certain measures taken by the European Union have direct application in Ireland.

The President is Head of State. The Office does not have executive functions and the President must generally act on the advice and authority of the Government. Dáil Éireann has 166 members called Teachtaí Dála (TDs) elected by universal suffrage (over 18s).

Seanad Éireann has 60 members. Eleven are nominated by the Taoiseach (Prime Minister), six elected by university graduates and forty-three elected by an electorate comprising national and local elected representatives. The powers of the Seanad as defined by the Constitution are, in general, less than those of the Dáil. In particular, it has no significant powers in relation to financial matters.

2.3 Court System

The basic structure of courts in Ireland has four levels, the District Court, the Circuit Court, the High Court and the Supreme Court. The District and Circuit

Courts are courts of local and limited jurisdiction established by statute law. The High Court is, by virtue of Article 34.3.1 of the Constitution, invested with full original jurisdiction in and power to determine all matters and questions whether of law or fact, civil or criminal. The Supreme Court is the court of final appeal and is established pursuant to Articles 34.2 and 34.4.1 of the Constitution. Judges in Ireland are independent both of the executive and the legislature and this independence is given full protection by the Constitution.

3. Legal or other measures adopted to implement the Convention

3.1 The formal equality in law of all citizens is set out in Article 40.1 of the Constitution. There has been universal adult suffrage in Ireland since the foundation of the State in 1922. Notwithstanding these facts Irish society had for the first fifty years of independence a very narrowly-focused and limiting view of women.

Over the past 25 years there has been an enormous improvement in the de jure and de facto equality of women with men in Irish society. This is attributable, broadly speaking, to three major factors:

- the growing worldwide consciousness of the rights of women;
- membership of the European Union and obligations deriving from this;
- a young well-educated population, ready and able to articulate its rights.

The legal, social and economic circumstances resulting from these factors are documented in detail in Ireland's first Report under the Convention. One interesting feature – indicative of the growing awareness by women of their own rights – is that some highly significant changes to the law came on foot of constitutional test cases taken by individual women.

The following mechanisms geared towards establishing equality between women and men are in place in Ireland.

3.2 Department of Equality and Law Reform

On 12 January, 1993, a Cabinet Minister was appointed as first ever Minister for Equality and Law Reform. He has responsibility for seeing that equality becomes a reality through institutional, administrative and legal reform. Among his other responsibilities the Minister exercises a monitoring and co-ordinating role on Government policies insofar as they affect women. A system has been set in train for all proposals coming to Government to be routinely scrutinised for their impact on women. There is a commitment to reach the target of a minimum of 40% female membership of each State Board.

Following a review of the existing employment equality legislation, the Anti-Discrimination (Pay) Act, 1974 and Employment Equality Act, 1977, options for enhancement of the legislation were identified and resulting proposals for amendment are before the Oireachtas. It is proposed to extend the legislation to prohibit discrimination in employment on a wide range of grounds including gender, marital status, family status, sexual orientation, religion, age, disability, race, colour, nationality, national or ethnic origin and membership of the Travelling community. The Unfair Dismissals (Amendment) Act, 1993 extended the categories of explicit protection from unfair dismissal to include age, sexual orientation and membership of the Travelling community.

Equal status legislation is being prepared which will prohibit discrimination in regard to education and access to goods, services and facilities and the disposal of accommodation or other premises, on grounds similar to the proposed employment equality legislation.

The Interpretation Act has been amended to provide for the use of the feminine gender in legislation and the legislation governing registration of births, deaths and marriages is being reviewed. In this context, an Act has been passed to provide for the removal of discrimination on the basis of gender in regard to the information recorded in the Register of Births.

The Department of Equality and Law Reform has responsibility in relation to a major programme of family law reform. Major updating of the law on the powers of the courts to deal with the financial consequences of marital breakdown in the context of judicial separations and where foreign decrees of separation and divorce are recognised in the State is contained in the Family Law Act, 1995. The same Act raised the age of marriage from 16 years to 18 years and provides for three months notice of marriage.

The Civil Legal Aid Act, 1995 gives a statutory framework to the State's scheme of civil legal aid and advice. The Domestic Violence Act, 1996 strengthens the powers of the courts to protect persons in the home from the violence of a spouse, partner or adult child and it strengthens the powers of the Garda Siochána (Police Force) to make arrests and to enter the family home. The Department is preparing proposals for legislation to update the law on guardianship of children, the evidence of children and on nullity of marriage as part of the process of reform of family law.

A referendum in 1995 resulted in the removal of the constitutional ban on divorce. The Family Law (Divorce) Act, 1996 makes provision for the exercise by the Courts of the jurisdiction newly conferred by the Constitution to grant decrees of divorce and enables the courts to make a wide range of property and financial orders in support of dependants.

3.3 Commission on the Status of Women

The Second (National) Commission on the Status of Women was established by the Government on 1 November, 1990 with the following terms of reference:

(i) to review the implementation of the recommendations of the first Commission on the Status of Women as set out in that Commission's report to the Minister for Finance in December, 1972;

(ii) to consider and make recommendations on the means, administrative and legislative, by which women will be able to participate on equal terms and conditions with men in economic, social, political and cultural life and, to this end, to consider the efficacy and feasibility of positive action measures;

(iii) in the context of (ii) above, to pay special attention to the needs of women in the home;

(iv) to establish the estimated costs of all recommendations made; and

(v) to report to the Government within a period of eighteen months from the date of its establishment.

The Commission's final Report, which proposed a major programme of reform, was presented to Government in January 1993.

The Report points out that in order for women to achieve equality there must be power sharing and partnership at the domestic level as well as at the level of the wider community. The Report drew a favourable response across the political spectrum and its recommendations will give an impetus to many legal and administrative reforms. Implementation is being monitored by the Department of Equality and Law Reform, assisted by a committee representative of women's organisations, Government departments and the social partners. Two reports charting progress in implementing the Commission's recommendations have been published. Up to the end of 1995 action had been taken in relation to 80% of the recommendations, with almost 47% implemented in full.[1]

---

1 Second Progress Report of the Monitoring Committee on the Implementation of the Recommendations of the Second Commission on the Status of Women.

4. Equality: enforcement procedures and mechanisms and the means used to promote the full development and advancement of women for the purpose of guaranteeing equal rights

4.1 The form and context of recent initiatives directed towards achieving equality in practice in Irish society are outlined in Part 2. In addition to those initiatives the following mechanisms also apply.

4.2 Fourth World Conference on Women

Ireland actively participated in preparations for the Fourth World Conference on Women and in the Conference itself.

The Irish delegation was headed by the Minister for Equality and Law Reform. Also present for parts of the Conference were the Minister for Education and the Minister of State at the Department of the Taoiseach. The delegation also included officials of the Departments of Equality and Law Reform, Foreign Affairs, Health and Education, four members of the Houses of the Oireachtas – three Deputies and a Senator – and representatives of the Employment Equality Agency, the National Economic and Social Forum, the National Women's Council of Ireland, the Irish Countrywomen's Association, Dóchas/Banúlacht (organisations involved with development issues) and the Irish Aid Advisory Committee.

In addition to providing funding for NGO representatives on the national delegation funding was given to other NGOs to assist them in sending representatives to the Conference and the NGO Forum.

Ireland accepted the text of the Platform for Action agreed at the Conference without reservations.

A report on progress made in implementing the Platform for Action was published in December, 1996. The report provides an overview of what is happening in Ireland and it is apparent from the report that the objectives and actions agreed at Beijing are being assimilated into all areas of Government policy in a manner appropriate to Irish conditions.

4.3 Employment Equality Agency

The Employment Equality Act, 1977 – which makes it unlawful to discriminate on grounds of sex or marital status in relation to recruitment for employment, conditions of employment, training or in the matter of opportunities for promotion – also provided for the establishment of an Employment Equality Agency (EEA). The EEA is a statutory body composed of a chairperson and ten ordinary members, including representatives of women's organisations, trade unions and employers. The members are appointed by the Minister for Equality and Law Reform for a term of five years.

The main functions of the EEA are:

- to work towards the elimination of discrimination in employment;
- to promote equality of opportunity in employment between men and women; and
- to keep under review the operation of the Anti-Discrimination (Pay) Act, 1974 and the Employment Equality Act, 1977 and, where necessary, to make proposals for amending either or both of those Acts.

The EEA provides an advisory and information service on equality legislation, represents individuals in cases arising under that legislation and promotes good practice at the level of the workplace.

While Equality Officers of the Labour Relations Commission and the Labour Court[2] have been assigned the main enforcement role under the Employment Equality Act, the EEA has certain enforcement functions also. It may conduct formal investigations and, if satisfied that there are practices or conduct which contravene the Anti-Discrimination (Pay) Act, 1974 or the Employment Equality Act, 1977, it can issue non-discrimination notices requiring that such practices cease. The EEA is empowered to seek a High Court injunction in respect of persistent discrimination.

Moreover, the EEA has the sole right to initiate proceedings in cases of the following:

- discriminatory advertisements;
- pressure on persons to discriminate; and
- where there is a general policy of discriminatory practices.

4.4 Oireachtas Joint Committee on Women's Rights

The Committee on Women's Rights, whose membership is drawn from both Houses of the Oireachtas, was first established in 1983 and has the following terms of reference:

(a) to examine or propose legislative measures which would materially affect the interests of women;

---

2 Equality Officers of the Labour Relations Commission investigate disputes in relation to alleged unlawful discrimination. The Commission, established under the Industrial Relations Act, 1990, promotes good industrial relations through the provision of conciliation and other services. Equality Officer recommendations may be appealed to the Labour Court which provides machinery for the formal investigation of industrial disputes.

(b) to consider means by which any areas of discrimination against women can be eliminated and by which the obstacles to their full participation in the political, social and economic life of the community can be removed;

(c) to consider specific economic and social disadvantages applying to women in the home and, bearing in mind the special nature of their contribution to the community, to recommend effective policy and administrative changes to help eliminate these disadvantages;

and to report to the Houses of the Oireachtas thereon.

4.5 National Economic and Social Forum

The National Economic and Social Forum (NESF), established in June, 1993, represents a new concept in participation in public affairs in Ireland. It is a consultative body which brings members of the Oireachtas and the social partners (i.e. trade unions, employers and farming organisations) together with representatives of women's organisations, the unemployed, disadvantaged and other groups who traditionally have been outside the consultation process. It aims to establish consensus on social and economic issues with a major focus on measures to tackle unemployment. Three of the Forum's 49 members represent the National Women's Council of Ireland (see 4.8 below). The Forum is chaired by a woman, appointed by the Government and women make up approximately 51% of the total membership.

4.6 Oireachtas Joint Committee on the Family

This Committee examines and reports on the impact of social change and State policies on the family, in both its extended and nuclear forms, with particular reference to the protection and enhancement of the interests of children and the elderly and measures which can be taken to support them, especially with regard to childcare, education, juvenile justice and care of the elderly.

The Joint Oireachtas Committee on the Family is expected to address the issue of the definition of the family.

4.7 Commission on the Family

The Commission on the Family was set up by the Minister for Social Welfare to examine the needs and priorities of the family in a rapidly changing social and economic environment.

The terms of reference for the Commission are wide-ranging and include:

- raising public awareness and improving understanding of issues affecting families;
- examining the effects of legislation and policies on families and making recommendations to the Government on proposals which would support and strengthen families;

- analysing recent economic and social changes affecting the position of families, taking account of relevant research already carried out;
- undertaking limited research as necessary.

The terms of reference also require that in carrying out its work the Commission, while having due regard to the provisions on the family in the Constitution intended to support the family unit, should reflect in its deliberations the definition of the family outlined by the United Nations.

It is expected to make proposals to the Oireachtas Joint Committee on the Family on any changes which it believes might be necessary in relation to the constitutional provisions on the family.

The Commission produced an Interim Report in November, 1996 and has been asked to make its final report to the Government by June 1997.

4.8 National Women's Council of Ireland (NWCI)

The National Women's Council of Ireland, formerly the Council for the Status of Women, was founded in 1973 to monitor implementation of the recommendations of the first national Commission on the Status of Women. It is an umbrella body which groups together approximately 150 NGOs representative of women's interests and concerns. It is recognised by Government as the body which puts forward women's concerns and perspectives. It receives almost all its core funding from the Government as a positive action measure. It is completely independent of Government on policy issues, answerable only to its own elected executive committee and members. In addition to its developmental role it is recognised as an informed and constructive critic of policy initiatives and its leaders enjoy ready access to senior politicians and policy makers.

The Council identifies core functions as lobbying Government, acting as a watchdog on equality issues, providing training and support for its members, changing societal attitudes on gender, linking and networking women's organisations within Ireland, north and south, the European Union through the European Women's Lobby and internationally.

The NWCI states that membership is open to all women's organisations or organisations which have a sizeable female membership. Organisations must be in existence for a year prior to applying for membership. From 1997 membership will be open to individuals.

Affiliated organisations are entitled to appoint two delegates to attend Council meetings, regardless of the size of the organisation. Delegates may be elected to the Executive Committee provided that they have been a delegate for at least a year.

5. Enforcement of the Convention

5.1 International human rights law in the Irish legal framework

Article 29.3 of the Constitution of Ireland states that

> *Ireland accepts the generally recognised principles of international law as its rule of conduct in its relations with other States.*

Ireland's legal system is a system of common law. Like other common law countries, Ireland has a "dualist" system under which international agreements to which Ireland becomes a party are incorporated into domestic law only by way of national legislation.

Where Ireland wishes to adhere to an international agreement it must ensure that domestic law is in conformity with the agreement in question. In some cases the entire contents of an international agreement have been transposed into domestic law by providing that the agreement shall have the force of law within the State. In other cases it is necessary to transpose only certain provisions of an agreement because other provisions are either already incorporated in domestic law or are of a nature not requiring incorporation. Sometimes it may be that for the same reason no transposition provisions are required at all.

The provisions of the Convention on the Elimination of All Forms of Discrimination Against Women are of a type covered for the most part by the fundamental rights provisions of the Irish Constitution. It would generally be inappropriate to make provision for fundamental rights by way of ordinary legislation which would be inferior and subject to existing constitutional provisions. The remedy of substituting the provisions of the Convention for the existing constitutional provision would be undesirable because it would involve jettisoning the jurisprudence built up around the existing provision. Finally, while it may appear that to have constitutional provisions in the precise terminology of the Convention would be legally advantageous, any advantage could be more apparent than real unless the domestic tribunal were to take the same view of its interpretation as the Committee on the Elimination of Discrimination Against Women. The solution of direct incorporation of the Convention into Irish law has not, therefore, been adopted.

Since our initial statement to CEDAW Ireland has acceded to the International Covenant on Civil and Political Rights, the International Covenant on Economic Social and Cultural Rights and the United Nations Convention on the Rights of the Child. Ireland has also ratified both optional protocols to the International Covenant on Civil and Political Rights.

Part 2

ARTICLE 1

For the purposes of the present Convention, the term "discrimination against women" shall mean any distinction, exclusion or restriction made on the basis of sex which has the effect or purpose of impairing or nullifying the recognition, enjoyment or exercise by women, irrespective of their marital status, on a basis of equality of men and women, of human rights and fundamental freedoms in the political, economic, social, cultural, civil or any other field.

Provisions exist both in the Irish Constitution and in legislation which give effect to this Article.

Article 40.1 of the Constitution states that:

> *All citizens shall, as human persons, be held equal before the law. This shall not be held to mean that the State shall not in its enactments have due regard to differences of capacity, physical and moral, and of social function.*

The guarantee provided by Article 40.1 has been interpreted in Irish case law as follows:

> *This provision is not a guarantee of absolute equality for all citizens in all circumstances but it is a guarantee of equality as human persons and (as the Irish language text of the Constitution makes quite clear) is a guarantee related to their dignity as human beings and a guarantee against any inequalities grounded upon an assumption, or indeed a belief, that some individual or individuals or classes of individuals, by reason of their human attributes or their ethnic or racial, social or religious background, are to be treated as the inferior or superior of other individuals in the community." (Quinns Supermarket v Attorney General, [1972]).*

Given this interpretation in case law, and the fact that several items of legislation dealing with equal pay, employment equality and equal treatment generally have been enacted the Government are satisfied that the reference to "social function" in the Constitution implies no obstacle to eliminating discrimination against women in Irish society.

The Review Group on the Constitution (see Part I, paragraph 2.1) recommended that Article 40.1 be amended to provide that

- all persons shall be held equal before the law. This shall not be taken to mean that the State may not have due regard to relevant differences.
- no person shall be unfairly discriminated against, either directly or indirectly, on any ground such as sex, race, age, disability, sexual orientation, colour, language, culture, religion, political or other opinion, national, social or ethnic origin, membership of the Travelling community, property, birth or other status.

The concept of discrimination has been defined in equality legislation, viz. the Anti-Discrimination (Pay) Act, 1974 and the Employment Equality Act, 1977 and in the Unfair Dismissals Acts, 1977 to 1995.

The Anti-Discrimination (Pay) Act, 1974 provides that:

> it shall be a term of the contract under which a woman is employed in any place that she shall be entitled to the same rate of remuneration as a man who is employed in that place by the same employer ... if both are employed on like work. (Section 2(1)).

The definition of discrimination enshrined in the 1974 Act makes no reference to marital status. It is designed to provide for equal treatment between men and women, regardless of their marital status. The Employment Equality Act, 1977 addressed the question of marital status as well as discrimination between men and women. It defines discrimination as follows:

(a) where by reason of her/his sex a person is treated less favourably than a person of the other sex;

(b) where because of her/his marital status a person is treated less favourably than another person of the same sex;

(c) where because of her/his sex or marital status a person is obliged to comply with a requirement, relating to employment or membership of a trade union, employer organisation or professional and/or trade body which is not an essential requirement for such employment or membership and in respect of which the proportion of persons of the other sex or (as the case may be) of a different marital status but of the same sex able to comply is substantially higher;

(d) where a person is penalised for having in good faith:
    (i) availed of the grievance procedures under the 1974 or 1977 Acts;
    (ii) opposed by lawful means an act which is unlawful under either Act;
    (iii) given evidence in any proceedings under either Act;
    (iv) given notice of an intention to do anything referred to in subparagraphs (i) to (iii) above.

The Unfair Dismissals Acts, 1977 to 1995 provide redress for employees who are unfairly dismissed from their employment. Among the grounds which the Acts stipulate that unfair dismissal is deemed to have taken place are:

- the employee's membership of a trade union;
- the religious or political opinions of the employee;
- the race or colour of the employee;
- the pregnancy of the employee or matters connected therewith;
- the exercise by an employee of her rights under the Maternity Protection Act, 1994;
- the age of an employee;
- membership of the Travelling community

- sexual orientation;
- legal proceedings against an employer where the employee is a party or a witness;
- unfair selection for redundancy;
- the exercise or contemplated exercise by an adopting parent of her right under the Adoptive Leave Act, 1995 to adoptive leave or additional adoptive leave.

ARTICLE 2

State Parties condemn discrimination against women in all its forms, agree to pursue by all appropriate means and without delay a policy of eliminating discrimination against women and, to this end undertake:

(a) *To embody the principle of the equality of men and women in their national constitutions or other appropriate legislation if not yet incorporated therein and to ensure, through law and other appropriate means, the practical realisation of this principle;*

(b) *To adopt appropriate legislative and other measures, including sanctions where appropriate, prohibiting all discrimination against women;*

(c) *To establish legal protection of the rights of women on an equal basis with men and to ensure through competent national tribunals and other public institutions the effective protection of women against any act of discrimination;*

(d) *To refrain from engaging in any act or practice of discrimination against women and to ensure that public authorities and institutions shall act in conformity with this obligation;*

(e) *To take all appropriate measures to eliminate discrimination against women by any person, organisation or enterprise;*

(f) *To take all appropriate measures, including legislation, to modify or abolish existing laws, regulations, customs and practices which constitute discrimination against women;*

(g) *To repeal all national penal provisions which constitute discrimination against women.*

(a) *To embody the principle of the equality of men and women in their national constitutions or other appropriate legislation if not yet incorporated therein and to ensure, through law and other appropriate means, the practical realisation of this principle.*

As outlined in the Commentary on Article 1, the principle of equality between women and men is enshrined in Article 40.1 of the Irish Constitution.

Article 41.2 of the Constitution of Ireland provides:

> *1. In particular the State recognises that by her life within the home woman gives to the State the support without which the common good cannot be achieved.*

2. *The State shall therefore endeavour to ensure that mothers shall not be obliged by economic necessity to engage in labour to the neglect of their duties in the home.*

This Article has been the subject of public debate in Ireland. It has been criticised because many people find the assumptions in the text objectionable but it has never, in fact, been judicially interpreted to justify discrimination against a woman. Others have praised the wording on the grounds that it gives strong support to the status of mothers who do not work outside the home. The (national) Second Commission on the Status of Women in its Report to Government of February 1993 recommended:

(a) deletion of article 41.2.2.; and

(b) that the Constitution should be amended to prohibit all forms of discrimination either direct or indirect based on sex.

The need for constitutional amendments as recommended by the Second Commission on the Status of Women was referred to the Constitution Review Group (see Part I, paragraph 2.1) for consideration.

The Review Group proposed the inclusion of a clause provided that no person should be discriminated against, directly or indirectly, on a number of grounds, including sex (see Commentary under Article 1). The Review Group considered whether Article 41.2 should be deleted or whether Section 2.1 should be retained in an amended form. The Review Group concluded that there should be constitutional recognition for the significant contribution made to society by the large group of people who provide a caring function within the home and recommended the retention of Article 41.2 in a gender neutral form, as follows:

- the State recognises that home and family life gives to society a support without which the common good cannot be achieved. The State shall endeavour to support persons caring for others within the home.

(b) To adopt appropriate legislative and other measures, including sanctions where appropriate, prohibiting all discrimination against women;

(c) To establish legal protection of the rights of women on an equal basis with men and to ensure through competent national tribunals and other public institutions the effective protection of women against any act of discrimination.

At present equality legislation in Ireland addresses conditions of employment and social welfare.

Paragraph 4.2 in Part 1 refers to the Employment Equality Agency and commentary under Article 1 refers to employment equality legislation.

As outlined in Part 1 of this Report the Irish Government is currently preparing comprehensive anti-discrimination legislation which will explicitly cover the categories of sex, marital status and family status. This legislation will considerably extend the equality legislation already in force relating to employment. Enhanced or augmented enforcement procedures and structures will be necessitated by the extended competence of equality legislation and will be provided for in the legislation.

(d) ***To refrain from engaging in any act or practice of discrimination against women and to ensure that public authorities and institutions shall act in conformity with this obligation;***

(e) ***To take all appropriate measures to eliminate discrimination against women by any person, organisation or enterprise.***

Legislation on equality applies equally to the public and private sector. The public sector has adopted additional positive action measures to complement the formal legislation on equality and the private sector is encouraged to do likewise.

The Civil Service, as an employer, is committed to equality of opportunity between women and men, irrespective of marital or family status. It is a policy of the Civil Service that the principles and practices of equal opportunity should apply to the recruitment, selection, placement, career development and all other conditions of service of civil servants.

Within the Civil Service, each Department has responsibility for implementing the Equal Opportunity Policy. Personnel Units are designated with specific responsibility for monitoring the effectiveness of the policy in their own Departments. The Department of Finance monitors the overall implementation of the policy across the Civil Service.

A national code of practice on sexual harassment, **Measures to Protect the Dignity of Women and Men at Work,** was published in September, 1994, following consultation with the social partners. The code will be promoted, reviewed and monitored by the Employment Equality Agency. While the present code is not mandatory the case for legal recognition for such a code is under consideration in the context of the current review of employment equality legislation.

A **'Statement of Equal Opportunity'** for the local authority and health service sectors has been in force since February 1990. The statement commits local authorities and health boards to treat and develop all their employees equally. The statement was agreed following negotiation between management and unions, and covers the areas of recruitment, selection, training and development, home and work, harassment and union/management responsibilities. A management team has been established to follow-up on equality matters in the local authority service.

The Local Appointments Commission is responsible for filling, by open competition, all permanent senior management and professional posts in the local authority and health service. The Commissioners are committed to a policy of equal opportunity.

Since 1991 the age limit for most public sector, including local authority, jobs has been raised to 50 years of age. This is intended to facilitate the entry or re-entry of full-time homemakers to the labour market.

(*f*) ***To take all appropriate measures, including legislation, to modify or abolish existing laws, regulations, customs and practices which constitute discrimination against women.***

A number of facilitating measures are set out under other articles of the Convention. Ireland's first Report under the Convention detailed the most important legislative initiatives to benefit women over the preceding thirty years. The following significant pieces of legislation have been enacted since examination of that Report.

Status of Children Act, 1987
This Act removed discrimination in the law against people born outside marriage, and has detailed provisions covering the areas of guardianship and maintenance of children, and succession rights. It also provides a court procedure for declarations of parentage and for the use of blood tests in civil proceedings involving questions of parentage.

Jurisdiction of Courts and Enforcement of Judgments (European Communities) Act, 1988
This Act enabled Ireland to ratify the 1968 E.C. Convention on Jurisdiction and the Enforcement of Judgments in Civil and Commercial Matters. While it is mainly concerned with commercial relationships, the Convention is important to women because it deals with maintenance matters. Under the Convention maintenance orders granted in one Contracting State are more or less automatically enforceable in all other Contracting States. In addition, a maintenance creditor (normally the wife) has a choice as to where she can sue for maintenance – either where she herself is domiciled or habitually resident or where the maintenance debtor is domiciled ('domiciled' under Irish law for the purposes of the Convention means ordinarily resident).

Family Law Act, 1988
This Act abolished the ancient action for restitution of conjugal rights.

Adoption (No. 2) Act, 1988
This Act extended the categories of children eligible for adoption to include certain children whose parents are married but have failed in their duty towards them.

Judicial Separation and Family Law Reform, 1989
The Act

(a) extends the grounds for granting a decree of judicial separation;

(b) empowers the court in separation proceedings to make orders for maintenance, secured maintenance, lump sum payments and orders in relation to property owned by either spouse; and

(c) provides for more informal hearings and the use of counselling and mediation services.

In exercising its powers to make financial provision and property orders the court must take into account all the circumstances of the case including a spouse's contribution in caring for the family and looking after the family home.

Criminal Law (Rape) (Amendment) Act, 1990

The Criminal Law (Rape) (Amendment) Act, 1990 represents a significant improvement in the legal protection afforded to victims of sexual assaults. The main provisions of the Act are:

- abolition of the rule that a husband cannot generally be found guilty of raping his wife;
- creation of two new offences of aggravated sexual assault and rape under Section 4 (to cater for offences involving sexual penetration which do not come within the traditional definition of rape), each with a maximum penalty of life imprisonment;
- extension of the special evidential and anonymity provisions (which previously applied only to rape victims) to all sexual assault victims.

The Act also provides for trials of rape and aggravated sexual assault to be held in the Central Criminal Court with the public but not the media being excluded.

Pensions Act, 1990

This Act provided for the equal treatment of women and men in occupational pension schemes.

Child Care Act, 1991

This Act represents a comprehensive and radical reform of the law in relation to the care and protection of children – especially those who have been assaulted, ill-treated, neglected, sexually abused or who are at risk.

The main provisions of the Act are:

(i) placement of a statutory duty on health boards to promote the welfare of children who are not receiving adequate care and protection;

(ii) strengthening the powers of health boards to provide child care and family support services;

(iii) improving procedures to facilitate immediate intervention by health boards and the Gardaí where children are in serious danger;

(iv) revising provisions to enable the courts to place children who have been assaulted, ill-treated, neglected, sexually abused or who are at risk in the care or under the supervision of health boards;

(v) introducing arrangements for the supervision and inspection of pre-school services such as nurseries, crèches, playgroups and other similar day care services; and

(vi) revising provisions in relation to the registration and inspection of residential centres for children.

The legislation was implemented on a phased basis, and was fully implemented by the end of 1996.

Child Abduction and Enforcement of Custody Orders Act, 1991
This Act enabled Ireland to ratify two international conventions concerning the abduction of children by parents across international frontiers, the Hague Convention on the Civil Aspects of International Child Abduction and the Council of Europe Convention on Recognition and Enforcement of Decisions concerning Custody of Children and on Restoration of Custody of Children.

Social Welfare Act, 1991
This Act provided for the extension of Social Insurance to anyone earning over £25 a week. This had the effect of bringing many part-time workers, mostly women, into the social security system. From April 1994 the amount increased to £30 a week.

Worker Protection (Regular Part-Time Employees) Act, 1991
This Act extended the scope of legislation regarding minimum notice, maternity leave, redress for unfair dismissal, worker participation, redundancy and insolvency payments protection and holiday entitlement to regular part-time employees. Regular part-time employees are defined as those who have worked at least thirteen weeks for an employer, work a minimum of eight hours per week and who prior to the enactment of this Act were excluded from the benefits of most employment legislation. The vast majority of part-time workers are women.

Criminal Evidence Act, 1992
This Act sets out the circumstances in which the spouse or former spouse of an accused person is competent and compellable to give evidence in criminal proceedings. The Act also makes it easier for witnesses to give evidence in criminal cases including physical or sexual abuse, by providing that in such cases witnesses' evidence may be given by live television link.

Unfair Dismissals (Amendment) Act 1993
This Act implemented a range of technical and administrative amendments to the Unfair Dismissals Act, 1977. The amended Act includes sexual orientation in the list of reasons for dismissal which are deemed to be automatically unfair.

Criminal Law (Sexual Offences) Act, 1993
The main purpose of this Act was to decriminalise homosexual acts between consenting adults. However, it also extended the law on soliciting in public, which previously applied only to prostitutes, to include clients of prostitutes and any third parties, such as pimps. The Act also strengthened the law on the protection of prostitutes from exploitation by introducing new offences aimed at the organisation and control of prostitution.

Criminal Justice Act, 1993
This Act enables unduly lenient sentences to be appealed and places an obligation on Courts, when determining sentences for sexual and violent offences, to take into account the effect on the victim. It also empowers the Court to order a convicted person to pay compensation to the victim.

Jurisdiction of Courts and Enforcement of Judgments Act, 1993
This Act enabled Ireland to ratify (a) the Convention on accession by Spain and Portugal to the EC Judgements Convention, and (b) the Lugano Convention (similar to the Judgements Convention) in respect of member States of the European Free Trade Association.

Interpretation (Amendment) Act, 1993
This Act provides that in the interpretation of legislation generally, unless the contrary intention appears, an expression in the feminine gender shall be construed as importing also the masculine gender. This means that the use of the feminine gender in legislation will no longer be confined to measures directed exclusively to women.

Maintenance Act, 1994
This Act enabled Ireland to ratify two international conventions (the Rome Convention and the New York Convention), both of which provide administrative assistance to maintenance creditors (usually women) who wish to recover maintenance from maintenance debtors who reside abroad.

Maternity Protection Act, 1994
This Act provides protection for all pregnant employees, employees who have recently given birth or who are breast feeding. It does so by giving them certain legal entitlements, the main ones being the right to 14 consecutive weeks maternity leave, the right to up to 4 weeks additional maternity leave, the right to return to work, the right to time off work without loss of pay to attend ante-natal and post-natal medical care appointments, the right to health and safety leave in certain circumstances, the right to protection of their jobs during maternity leave, additional maternity leave, health and safety leave and time off for ante-natal and post-natal care and the right not to be dismissed for any pregnancy related reason from the beginning of pregnancy until the end of maternity leave. Fathers are entitled to avail of periods of leave in certain limited circumstances under this Act.

The Act also provides a mechanism for the processing of disputes and appeals concerning certain entitlements arising out of provisions of the legislation.

Adoptive Leave Act, 1995
This Act provides an entitlement to a minimum period of 10 weeks adoptive leave for female employees. Adoptive leave is also available to males in certain limited circumstances.

Criminal Law (Incest Proceedings) Act, 1995
This Act provides that while members of the public shall be excluded from incest proceedings the press shall be entitled to attend and to report on such proceedings subject to a requirement that no information be published which would enable an incest victim to be identified. In addition, the Act increased to life imprisonment the maximum penalty to which a person convicted of incest can be sentenced.

Family Law Act, 1995
This Act enables the court to make maintenance, pension, property and other ancillary orders in cases where foreign decrees of divorce and judicial separation are entitled to recognition in the State; it repeals and re-enacts with amendments the powers of the courts to make orders in support of spouses and children in separation proceedings; it empowers the court to make declarations in relation to the status of a person's marriage; it raises the minimum age for marriage from 16 years to 18 years and provides for three months notice of marriage; it gives a statutory role to welfare services in family law cases; it strengthens the enforcement powers of the court in relation to maintenance and also widens the court's powers to order lump sum payments in addition to or in substitution for periodic payments (not just in separation proceedings as heretofore).

Social Welfare Act, 1995
This Act provides for budgetary improvements, miscellaneous changes in the Social Welfare code and the introduction of Adoptive Benefit to provide for people taking leave under the Adoptive Leave Act, 1995.

Social Welfare (No. 2) Act, 1995
This Act ensures that divorced people will not be disadvantaged in terms of their social welfare entitlements.

Health and Safety Benefit Regulations 1994 and 1995
A Health and Safety Benefit was first legislated for in 1994. It is a social insurance payment and is now available to pregnant and nursing mothers who get Health and Safety Leave if they are exposed to specified risks at work or working nightshift hours.

Social Welfare Act, 1996
Apart from providing for budgetary increases, this Act introduces a new One-Parent Family Payment to replace the Deserted Wife's Benefit and Lone Parent Allowance and transfers responsibility for Disabled Person's Maintenance Allowance (to be renamed Disability Allowance) from the Department of Health to the Department of Social Welfare. The Act also provides for a number of other miscellaneous changes in the Social Welfare Code.

Civil Legal Aid Act, 1995
This Act put the State's scheme of civil legal aid and advice on a statutory basis.

Domestic Violence Act, 1996
This Bill strengthens the powers of the courts to protect persons from domestic violence, extends those powers to protect cohabitants and strengthens also the powers of arrest of the Garda Siochána (Police Force).

Fifteenth Amendment of the Constitution Act, 1996
This Act contains the text of the amendment of the Constitution which confers jurisdiction on courts to grant decrees of divorce. That text was approved by the people in the referendum held in November, 1995.

Family Law (Divorce) Act, 1996
This Act details extensive powers which the courts have to make orders in support of spouses and children in or after proceedings for divorce. The Act comes into operation on 27 February, 1997.

Civil Liability (Amendment) Act, 1996
This Bill extends to co-habitants and persons whose foreign divorce is entitled to recognition in Ireland the right to claim certain damages when the other co-habitant or former spouse is fatally injured because of the wrongful act of a person.

(g) To repeal all national penal provisions which constitute discrimination against women.

There are no such provisions under Irish criminal law.

ARTICLE 3

States Parties shall take in all fields, in particular in the political, social, economic and cultural fields, all appropriate measures, including legislation, to ensure the full development and advancement of women, for the purpose of guaranteeing them the exercise and enjoyment of human rights and fundamental freedoms on a basis of equality with men.

The Constitution of Ireland is based on an underlying philosophy of equality between men and women. As outlined under Article 1, Article 40.1 of the Constitution guarantees equality before the law. In addition, Article 40.3.1 guarantees that the State shall respect and, as far as possible, by its laws defend and vindicate the personal rights of the citizen.

Part I of this Report sets out the general situation regarding the political, social and economic fields. The commentary on Article 1 sets out the national machinery in operation for the promotion of equality of opportunity between women and men. The commentary on Article 2 sets out specific legislative measures taken to enhance women's position in economic and social life.

INITIATIVES

The following specific initiatives intended to promote the rights of women are also important.

Report of the Second (national) Commission on the Status of Women
The Second (national) Commission on the Status of Women has already been referred to in Part 1. In preparing its Report, the Commission invited submissions from the public and consulted widely with Government Departments, statutory and voluntary bodies, women's organisations and research institutes.

The Commission's Report contains 210 separate recommendations on action to improve the situation of women in Ireland. The Report deals with the following areas:

- constitutional and legal issues;
- women in the home;
- employment;
- childcare;
- women in situations of disadvantage;
- rural women;
- participation in politics and public life;
- culture and sport;

- education;
- training and labour market initiatives;
- health.

The Government is committed to a programme of reform to implement recommendations drawn from the Commission's Report. See Part 1, paragraph 3.3.

Gender proofing Government policies

In recent years there has been a general recognition that policy initiatives proposed by Government need to be gender proofed, i.e. assessed for the differential effect they have on women and men. This is because a policy initiative which in itself seems neutral as between women and men may not be so in practice because it is based on structures and situations where women are under-represented or exist primarily as dependants. Gender proofing is intended to overcome the potential for indirect discrimination and to contribute towards an integrated equal opportunities policy.

The Government decided in February, 1993 that all policy proposals put forward for decision by Government should include an assessment of the probable impact on women of the proposed policy change.

Interpretation (Amendment) Act, 1993

The *Interpretation Act*, passed in 1937, defines the meaning and construction of words and expressions used in Bills and Acts of the Oireachtas (parliament) and in the instruments made under these Acts.

Section 11(b) of the Act reads as follows:

> Masculine and Feminine
> Every word importing the masculine gender shall, unless the contrary intention appears, be construed as if it also imported the feminine gender.

The *converse* of this did not apply. There was no provision in the Act for being able to construe the feminine gender as also importing to the masculine with the consequence that it was not possible to use the feminine gender in Acts or instruments of the Oireachtas which primarily affected women. The Government decided that the Interpretation Act should be amended to provide that:

- Bills and Statutory Instruments shall be framed in gender neutral language;
- references primarily directed at men may be framed in the masculine; and
- references primarily directed at women may be framed in the feminine.

The Interpretation (Amendment) Act, 1993 was passed accordingly.

The position in relation to particular groups of vulnerable women is as follows.

Lone Parents

The vast majority of lone parent families are headed by women. A greater proportion of lone mothers in Ireland are economically active in comparison to other mothers. The Lone Parent Allowance from the Department of Social Welfare is payable if a person is bringing up one or more children without the support of a partner, subject to a means test.

Lone parents in receipt of a Lone Parents' Allowance benefit from incentives to encourage their participation in the labour market. In 1994 the amount of earnings disregarded in determining entitlement to social welfare were increased and lone parents are being allowed to retain a greater proportion of their Lone Parents' Allowance while working. Working lone parents are also eligible for Family Income Supplement, which is not counted as income for means test purposes. Lone parents in receipt of Lone Parents' Allowance are eligible to participate in Community Employment, which is the main employment scheme directed at persons who are long-term unemployed.

In addition, lone parents in employment, subject to being in receipt of a social welfare widow's pension or medical card are exempt from the health contribution and the employment training levy.

The Minister for Social Welfare is to introduce a new One-Parent Family Payment to replace the existing arrangements for lone parents from early 1997 which will

- be non-discriminatory in the treatment of men and women rearing children on their own;
- be non-judgemental in that the requirement to prove desertion is being dispensed with in the social welfare system.

The new payment will incorporate the existing means-tested scheme for lone parents as well as the deserted wives benefit scheme. It will enable people who are bringing up children on their own, the majority of whom are women, to have earnings within certain limits and retain their allowance. This will serve to encourage the participation of lone parents in the labour force.

Women will no longer be required to prove desertion which will dispense with the intrusive questioning which establishing desertion necessitates, at a particularly vulnerable time in their lives.

A Scheme of Grants for Lone Parents to assist them return to work or take up second chance education opportunities is also in operation. Grants may be made to lone parents support and self-help groups and other groups who work with lone parents.

TRAVELLER WOMEN

Travellers, as a group, are particularly affected by poverty. Traveller women have a higher mortality rate, lower life expectancy and stillbirth and infant mortality rates almost three times that of the population of Ireland as a whole. This pattern of ill health is compounded by high rates of illiteracy, poor living conditions and heavy domestic responsibilities.

The provision of proper accommodation for the Travelling community in houses or serviced caravan sites, according to the wishes of the Travelling community themselves has been Government policy for over twenty years.

The Minister for Equality and Law Reform established a Task Force on the Travelling Community in July, 1993 to advise and report on the needs of Travellers and on Government policy generally in relation to the Travelling community, in a range of areas such as accommodation, health, equality, education and training.

The Task Force issued an interim report in January, 1994 and published its final report July, 1995. The Report of the Task Force was the first comprehensive review of the needs of the Traveller community since the Report of the Travelling People Review Body published in 1983.

The Report of the Task Force examined and made recommendations in relation to three principal areas:

- key issues of relevance to Travellers, including Traveller women, namely, accommodation, access to health services, education and training provision and economic development and employment, including the co-ordination of approaches by the relevant statutory agencies whose services impact on members of the Travelling community;
- relationships between Travellers and settled people;
- the experience of Travellers with a particular focus on culture and discrimination.

The Report also examined mechanisms for facilitating improved relationships between the Traveller and settled communities, particularly at local level and made recommendations with a view to reducing conflict and strengthening mutual respect and understanding which it is hoped will merge into, what the Task Force calls, a Strategy for Reconciliation.

In addition to a separate chapter with a number of recommendations aimed at improving the position of Traveller women in Irish society, (e.g. provision of childcare facilities, initiatives to deal with domestic violence and access to training and economic opportunities), many of the recommendations in other chapters of the Report of the Task Force also deal with issues of concern to Traveller women e.g. education, health, discrimination, accommodation etc.

As the Report of the Task Force impacts on a wide range of policy areas which are the responsibility of a number of Ministers, the Government established an Inter-Departmental Working Group to consider the implementation of the Report including, in particular, the costs involved. The Report of the Inter-Departmental Working Group was considered by Government in March, 1996 when it approved a comprehensive package of actions and services relating to the Travelling community.

Under the NOW European Community Initiative (see Article 4) two projects are specifically targeted at the needs of Traveller women.

The over-riding goal of training centres operated by FÁS (the national training authority) for Travellers is to help them to develop their full potential, to break the cycle of illiteracy and social deprivation in which they are trapped and to enable them to become, as soon as possible, self-reliant and self-supporting members of society. The training centres provide a combination of training in life skills and in basic manual skills together with a considerable input in the area of literacy and numeracy. The training lasts for forty-eight weeks.

Women with Disabilities

The Commission on the Status of People with Disabilities was established in 1993 by the Minister for Equality and Law Reform. People with disabilities, their advocates and parents made up 60% of the membership of the Commission. Over 40% of the members were women and as part of its consultative programme a consultation exercise was organised for women with disabilities in conjunction with the National Women's Council of Ireland.

The Report of the Commission on the Status of People with Disabilities was published in November, 1996. This Report is the first ever in-depth examination of the situation of people with disabilities in Ireland and impacts on a range of policy issues which are the responsibility of many Government Departments and agencies.

The Commission estimates that at least 5% (150,000) of the population are women with disabilities. The Report states that women with disabilities encounter "double disadvantage" both as people with a disability and as women with a disability. Women with disabilities are still not included in the decision-making processes, policy making and political structures of government and are under-represented in the decision-making structures of voluntary organisations, even those which provide support for people with conditions which affect more women than men.

The Commission believes that no woman's experience of disability should render her powerless in relation to the basic rights of all women. Women with disabilities must be consulted in developing policies for them and they should be provided with sufficient resources to maintain their status within the family and within the local community. The Commission asks that policy makers and others be informed and be aware of the issues arising from women's experience of disability, based on the social understanding of disability rather than relying on the medical and individualistic model of disability.

The Irish Government has given approval for the preparation of a plan of action arising from the Report. It is intended to establish a Monitoring Committee, comprising organisations representing people with disabilities, their families and carers and service providers as well as social partners and Government Departments, to monitor the implementation of the Commission's recommendations.

The Housing Acts, 1966 to 1992 are general in nature and as such relate to persons with disabilities in the same way as everyone else. However, a specific provision in these acts requires housing authorities to identify the 'disabled/handicapped' as a separate category in their assessments of need for local authority housing.

Lesbian Women

Lesbian women can be faced with the double disadvantage of gender specific difficulties and discrimination on the basis of sexual orientation. On the evidence of the 1990 European Values Study, Irish attitudes are consistently less tolerant than the EU average with regard to sexual orientation. However, it should be noted that, when compared to previous European Values Studies, the trend in Ireland is towards a more liberal attitude on homosexuality, with women being slightly more liberal than men.

The Criminal Law (Sexual Offences) Act, 1993 decriminalised homosexual acts between consenting male adults. Lesbian acts never constituted a criminal offence.

New legislation that will prohibit discrimination in employment and non-employment on a wide range of grounds is under preparation. It is proposed that sexual orientation will be among the prohibited grounds for discrimination under the legislation. The Unfair Dismissals (Amendment) Act, 1993 specifically prohibits the dismissal of an employee on grounds of sexual orientation. Lesbian partners are in the same situation as unmarried heterosexual cohabitees in that their relationship does not have legal status.

LOT (Lesbians Organising Together) received a grant of £10,000 in 1995 under the Department of Social Welfare scheme of grants for women's groups. Further funding of £20,000 per year was allocated for 1996 and 1997.

Equality in the Cultural Field

Funding for the contemporary arts is administered by the Arts Council, a body established by the Oireachtas to stimulate public interest in the arts, to promote the knowledge, appreciation and practice of the arts, and to assist in improving standards.

The Arts Council is committed to the ideal of a society based on principles of equality and equal opportunity. It is a condition of grant aid that organisations assisted by the Council agree to avoid any form of discriminatory practice.

The Arts Council recently published "The Arts Plan 1995-1997" to reflect the current Government's commitment to a planned approach to the development of arts and culture in Ireland, based on extensive public consultation. A key strategic objective of the plan is **Access**, designed "to encourage real participation in the arts in terms of availability and access, with particular reference to young people, children, and people with disabilities and taking account of social as well as geographical barriers". Although not explicitly stated, this strategic objective implicitly offers assurances concerning the principle of access to arts and cultural activities for both genders.

The Minister for Arts, Culture and the Gaeltacht launched a Cultural Development Incentive Scheme which is designed to establish a network of arts and cultural capital infrastructure, notably in the regions outside Dublin. Some £23 million is being allocated towards this scheme in the period to 1999. This infrastructure will greatly facilitate access by the Irish population to cultural expression and activity and the principle of equality of access for both women and men will be assured in all new arrangements.

ARTICLE 4

(1) ***Adoption by States Parties of temporary special measures aimed at accelerating de facto equality between men and women shall not be considered as discrimination defined in the present Convention, but shall in no way entail as a consequence the maintenance of unequal or separate standards; these measures shall be discontinued when the objectives of equality of opportunity and treatment have been achieved.***

(2) ***Adoption by States Parties of special measures, including those measures contained in the present Convention, aimed at protecting maternity shall not be considered discrimination.***

In Ireland, provisions authorising positive action to redress previous inequality are not considered to be in conflict with the general principle of equality between men and women. Thus, Section 15 of the Employment Equality Act, 1977, provides that it shall not be unlawful for any person

- to arrange for or provide training for persons of a particular sex in a type, form or category of work in which either no, or an insignificant number, of persons of that sex had been engaged in the period of twelve months ending at the commencement of the training; or
- to encourage persons of that sex to take advantage of opportunities for doing such work.

Special measures taken in the field of education are outlined in the commentary under Article 10 of the Convention.

In 1990, FÁS, the National Training Authority, initiated a Positive Action Programme for Women, which aims to promote the participation by women in non-traditional and growing sectors of the labour market. It encompasses positive action measures in all areas of FÁS activity and establishes annual targets to be achieved in key areas such as selected specific skills courses, preparatory and pre-apprenticeship training, the community youth training programme and the social employment scheme. The results of equality initiatives are monitored by means of an annual report.

Women accounted for 42.2% of all FÁS trainees in 1995. This compares with a figure of 36.5% participation by women in the labour force in the same year.

The Commentary under Article 11.1 (d) includes details of FÁS Positive Action in Training.

In the field of employment a range of equal opportunities policies are implemented, particularly in the public sector. An equal opportunities policy is intended to complement rights in law through such means as tackling inequalities generated by past discrimination, overcoming structural barriers and promoting specific measures to enable the potential of all employees to be realised.

Both the Irish Business and Employers' Confederation and the Irish Congress of Trade Unions have guidelines on equal opportunities. In 1992, the Employment Equality Agency published a model equal opportunities policy to assist employers in drawing up an equal opportunities policy.

Civil Service

Ireland's First Report included details of the Equal Opportunities Policy and Guidelines for the Civil Service, published in 1986. A copy of the Policy and Guidelines booklet is given to all new entrants to the Civil Service. The Commentary under Article 5(a) includes information on developments since Ireland's First Report and action to eliminate sexism and sex stereotyping in the Civil Service.

The implementation of the equal opportunities policy in the civil service is monitored by the Department of Finance in close consultation with the civil service trade unions. An annual report is produced and distributed to all Departments.

Promotion and Recruitment

Promotion and recruitment competitions for appointments in the civil service are open to both men and women. Advertisements and circulars announcing external and internal competitions indicate clearly that the civil service is committed to a policy of equal opportunity. Upper age limits for general recruitment to the civil service were raised substantially, to age 50, in 1991. This is of particular benefit for women who wish to join, or return to, the labour market.

Members of interview boards convened by the Civil Service Commission are briefed on the civil service policy in relation to equality of opportunity and in addition are provided with written guidelines stating the policy in relation to the conduct of interviews. Statistics relating to the candidature and outcome of recruitment and promotion competitions and membership of interview boards are analysed and included in the annual report referred to above.

Since 1985, competitions have been held for appointments at Secretary and Assistant Secretary levels, that is at the most senior levels in the Civil Service. The competitions (usually an interview) are run by the Top Level Appointments Committee. The Committee has five members, currently four men and one woman.

Other initiatives

Up to 1994, a three day training programme was offered to women in management grades by the Civil Service training body, the Centre for Management and Organisation Development. Participants on this programme had the option of becoming part of a Women Managers' Network on completion of the course. In 1995 it was decided to discontinue the standard training programme and to expand the activities of the Network to encompass training events, presentations by expert speakers and initiatives to promote equality throughout the Civil Service. Membership of the Network was opened to all interested women managers and there are currently over 200 members.

This framework is complemented by a number of family-friendly policies such as flexible working hours, career breaks and job-sharing. A crèche for the children of civil servants opened in April, 1992.

Scheme of Grants for Local Women's Groups

Another important empowerment and positive action measure is provided by the Department of Social Welfare's Scheme of Grants for Locally based Women's Groups. The scheme provides support and assistance to these groups to encourage self-help and personal development for women working in the home, to provide educational opportunities, to encourage the active participation of women in the group and in their community and to help address social problems such as stress and isolation. In allocating grants, priority is given to groups in disadvantaged areas and to projects catering mainly for disadvantaged groups. The majority of the groups funded are completely dependent on the unpaid work of local women. Both rural and urban women benefit from these grants.

Analysis to date shows that the scheme has proved very beneficial to the many women involved in the programmes and that the scheme is highly cost-effective from the State's point of view as a development and support strategy.

Many of the groups funded under the Scheme developed to the stage where they provide services to a wider group of women and could benefit from the security of continuity of funding. A programme was established in 1994 whereby guaranteed funding over a three year period would be provided to a number of the more developed groups enabling them to expand their work and to plan their activities more effectively.

A Scheme of Grants for Lone Parents to assist them return to work or take up second chance educational opportunities is also in operation. Grants may be made to lone parents support and self-help groups and other groups who work with lone parents. Grants are now provided for the support of locally based men's groups. Grants may be paid for a wide range of activities covering almost every aspect of personal and skills development for men.

New Opportunities for Women

The NOW Programme (New Opportunities for Women) was a European Union initiative which promoted equality for women in vocational training and employment. NOW formed an integral part of the implementation of the EC Commission's Third Medium-Term programme on Equal Opportunities (1991-1995).

The programme was intended to contribute to the integration of women into the labour market through the following actions:

- improvement in the quality of employment through training;
- overcoming obstacles to access and participation in training and employment by women;
- promotion of entrepreneurial and local employment initiatives.

NOW funded actions by voluntary groups, women's groups and public and statutory agencies. It encouraged both the voluntary and private sectors to work together with public and statutory agencies. It is hoped that the synergy created will provide new ways of facilitating women's access to training, employment and enterprise creation. Expenditure over the life time of the programme was £7m and 32 projects were assisted.

NOW 1995-1999

In this round of EU funds, NOW is an integral part of the EU Employment Initiative which comprises HORIZON (disability), HORIZON (disadvantage) and Youthstart. Its actions will focus on priority areas identified by the Fourth Community Action Programme on Equal Opportunities between Women and Men. These priorities include reconciliation of working and family life, desegregation of the labour market, access to education and training, and a balanced representation of women and men in decision-making.

A critical objective of NOW in Ireland is to develop gender equality systems and practices for the public and private sectors to enable these organisations to monitor and review practices and improve participation rates of women at all levels. Another priority of NOW is to pilot innovative actions that support the increased participation of women in business creation and in local decision-making structures. Access and Information and Guidance Services particularly for women who are marginalised from labour market services, e.g. Traveller women and other disadvantaged groups are another priority. It is envisaged that the integration of successful outcomes from such projects into national systems of training and employment will have a long-term impact on labour market provision. The mainstreaming of the good practices developed is the underlying goal of Employment NOW.

All NOW projects ensure the full participation of women and include flexibility in delivery and design and the provision of support services that facilitate the full take up of actions by women.

Action for Equality Awards

The Minister for Labour (now Equality and Law Reform) and the Employment Equality Agency jointly organised the Equality Focus Award Scheme in 1990 and 1992. The Scheme was designed to recognise good employment practices in the equal opportunities area. Employers in the public and private sector were eligible to compete in various categories based on size.

As a further development of this award scheme the Department of Equality and Law Reform, in co-operation with the social partners and other interested bodies, developed the "Action for Equality Awards". The purpose of this awards scheme is to recognise good equality practices in Irish society. Awards were made in 1996 for achievement in promoting equality in two categories – initiatives in the workplace and initiatives in other areas. Individuals, employers, providers of a service, local authorities, schools and voluntary bodies could be nominated. Finalists featured in a four-part television series shown on the national television channel at prime time in September, 1996. The Awards were co-sponsored by the Department and the national broadcasting authority, RTÉ.

Provisions for the protection of maternity are outlined in the commentary under Article 11.2. Information on other protective legislation is provided under Article 11.1 (a) and (b).

ARTICLE 5

State Parties shall take all appropriate measures:

(a) To modify the social and cultural patterns of conduct of men and women, with a view to achieving the elimination of prejudices and customary and all other practices which are based on the idea of the inferiority or the superiority of either of the sexes or on stereotyped roles of men and women;

(b) To ensure that family education includes proper understanding of maternity as a social function and the recognition of the common responsibility of men and women in the upbringing and development of their children, it being understood that the interest of the children is the primordial consideration in all cases.

(a) To modify the social and cultural patterns of conduct of men and women, with a view to achieving the elimination of prejudices and customary and all other practices which are based on the idea of the inferiority or the superiority of either of the sexes or on stereotyped roles of men and women.

It is recognised that to achieve de facto as well as de jure equality between women and men it is necessary to change attitudes and cultural conditioning. The importance of legislative and administrative change should not be underestimated in bringing about attitudinal change.

Part 1 and the Commentary on Article 3 refers to the establishment of the Second (National) Commission on the Status of Women in 1990. The Terms of Reference of the Commission included, inter alia:

> to consider and make recommendations on the means, administrative and legislative, by which women will be able to participate on equal terms and conditions with men in economic, social, political and cultural life and, to this end, to consider the efficacy and feasibility of positive action measures.

The Report of the Commission points out that despite the progress made over the last twenty years towards equal opportunities the onus for behavioural modification to date has been overwhelmingly on women. Participation by women in paid employment has not been matched by more equal sharing of family responsibilities. A Eurobarometer[1] study makes it plain that this is to varying degrees a Europe-wide problem, if not a worldwide one.

The Commission on the Status of Women believed that there were structural and attitudinal reasons why women are not included more in political life, including limiting social values, difficulties in devoting themselves simultaneously to family life, paid employment and political tasks and the ongoing reluctance of political parties to select women candidates.

---

1 Eurobarometer 34 Study on Family and Work, published in December, 1992.

Part 1 of this Report refers to the establishment of the Department of Equality and Law Reform. Two key pieces of legislation in the equality area are priorities for the Department:

(i) reform of the employment equality legislation, taking into account the case law the existing Acts have given rise to and any perceived shortcomings or anomalies they contain and the extension of the protection of the Acts to additional categories, including family status;

(ii) introduction of equal status legislation to prohibit discrimination in non-employment areas e.g. goods, facilities, services, education. This will facilitate the withdrawal of Ireland's reservation in relation to Article 13(b) and (c) and will bring about social and cultural change.

EDUCATION

Initiatives have been taken in the field of education to modify social and cultural patterns of conduct which are derived from stereotypical views of the roles of women and men in society. These are dealt with under Article 10.

The Employment Equality Agency, with support and advice from the Department of Education, the National Council for Curriculum and Assessment and St Patrick's Teacher Training Centre produced a video and related materials for use in primary schools to highlight and challenge stereotypical assumptions about gender roles.

ADVERTISING

There is no legislation relating to the portrayal of women in advertising at present. The Advertising Standards Authority for Ireland (ASAI) operates a Code of Advertising Standards, which seeks to guard against misrepresentation and exploitation in advertising. The Authority is a voluntary, self regulatory body which is endorsed by the Director of Consumer Affairs, an officer charged by the Oireachtas to oversee Ireland's consumer protection legislation.

The ASAI completed a review of the Code of Advertising Standards in 1995. This review involved consultation with over 70 organisations representing commercial and business interests, consumer organisations, representatives of women's interests, professional and trade organisations, regulatory agencies and Government Departments. On the basis of this review and the extensive consultation undertaken, ASAI is satisfied about the effectiveness of the self-regulatory system in advertising and sales promotion including the record of acceptance of ASAI adjudications by the advertising industry.

Rules about taste and decency discourage advertisements that may offend under a range of headings including considerations of age, disability, gender, race, religion, sex or sexual orientation. Increased emphasis is placed on the principle of equality of men and women and the avoidance of sexism and stereotyping.

RTE, the national television and radio authority, has a Code of Standards for Broadcast Advertising. This Code draws advertisers' attention to the need to take cognisance of the changing role of women in Irish society.

Codes of standards, practice and prohibitions in advertising, sponsorship and other forms of commercial promotion in broadcasting services were drawn up by the Minister for Arts, Culture and the Gaeltacht under the Broadcasting Act, 1990 and published in September, 1995. The codes provide, inter alia, that broadcast advertising shall not prejudice respect for human dignity or include any discrimination on grounds of race, sex or nationality.

Action to eliminate sexism and sex-stereotyping in the Civil Service

Ireland's First Report referred to the introduction of the Equal Opportunity Policy and Guidelines for the Civil Service. Developments since then have included the following:

- the establishment of a section within the Department of Finance (which is responsible for personnel matters in the Civil Service) with special responsibility for gender equality policy;
- the setting up of the Equal Opportunities Sub-Committee comprising management and staff side interests which overviews progress on the implementation of the Policy and Guidelines and considers a wide range of equality issues;
- the development of a network of women managers in the Civil Service which has the threefold aim of (i) providing training which meets the members' specific interests and needs, (ii) enabling women managers to build contacts and share knowledge across Government Departments, and (iii) promoting debate and initiatives on equality issues throughout the Civil Service;
- specific equal opportunity training programmes for line managers/supervisors at departmental level and the incorporation of equal opportunity training and awareness into certain general management courses and selection interview skills courses;
- regular reviews of training material to ensure that it is consistent with equal opportunity policy;
- the formal introduction of non-discriminatory forms of address for official purposes;
- monitoring of the composition of interview boards, with particular emphasis on the inclusion of women as members of such boards;
- the implementation of guidelines for dealing with complaints of sexual harassment in the work place.

CULTURE

The principle of **Access**, which is a key strategic objective of the Arts Council's "The Arts Plan 1995-1997" together with the Cultural Development Incentive Scheme up to the year 1999 (see commentary on Article 3), will contribute greatly to the modification of cultural patterns of conduct of women and men. The flourishing of arts and cultural activity which these measures will facilitate will, it is considered, fully respond to the objectives of this Article.

(b) ***To ensure that family education includes proper understanding of maternity as a social function and the recognition of the common responsibility of men and women in the upbringing and development of their children, it being understood that the interest of the children is the primordial consideration in all cases.***

Through initiatives to eliminate sex stereotyping in schools and through adult education, an attempt has been made to help break down traditional barriers to the realisation of equality both in the work place and in the home. Further details on these measures are given in the commentary under Article 10.

Plans are well advanced for the introduction of a programme of Relationships and Sexuality Education into all schools. The programme will, inter alia:

- promote knowledge of and respect for reproduction;
- enable students to value family life and appreciate the responsibilities of parenthood.

The National Council for Curriculum and Assessment has a special remit to ensure that sexism and sex stereotyping is eliminated from curricula in primary and second level schools and to work towards the implementation of gender equality in schools. The new programmes being introduced in the Senior Cycle in schools contain a large element of preparation for life, including the recognition of the equal responsibilities of men and women.

There are a number of programmes supported by the Health Promotion Unit of the Department of Health which address relationships and sexuality education in the context of a broad health education programme. These programmes seek to promote responsibility in the area of sexual health. The Unit has supported the Eastern Health Board in a pilot programme aimed specifically at reducing teenage pregnancies. The Unit is also working with the Department of Education with a view to further development and dissemination of good practice in relationships and sexuality education in the school setting.

Article 6

State Parties shall take all appropriate measures, including legislation, to suppress all forms of traffic in women and exploitation of prostitution of women.

Under Irish law, prostitution is not in itself an offence, but the law does seek to protect prostitutes from exploitation and to protect the public from certain public manifestations of prostitution.

It is an offence for a person, in a street or public place, to solicit or importune another person for the purposes of prostitution. The offence applies equally to a prostitute (male or female) soliciting a client, a client soliciting a prostitute, or a third party soliciting one on behalf of the other. The same offence and penalties apply to prostitutes, clients or anyone who solicits in a public place.

It is also an offence to solicit or importune another person in order to commit certain sexual offences, such as sexual relations with under-age persons, to keep or manage a brothel, or to allow premises to be used as a brothel.

A member of the Garda Síochána (police force) who has reasonable cause to suspect that a person is loitering in a street or public place in order to solicit for the purposes of prostitution may direct that person to leave the scene immediately. It is an offence not to comply with such a direction without reasonable cause. "Loitering" includes loitering in a motor vehicle and this provision therefore applies to kerb-crawlers.

In relation to the exploitation of prostitutes and the organisation of prostitution it is an offence for a person, for gain, to compel or coerce another person to be a prostitute or, for gain, to control or direct a prostitute or to organise prostitution. It is also an offence for a person knowingly to live on the earnings of a prostitute and to aid and abet that prostitution.

Statistics in relation to criminal charges under the Criminal Law (Sexual Offences) Act, 1993 are set out in table 6.1.

Table 6.1

Criminal Law (Sexual Offences) Act, 1993

FOR THE PERIOD 7 JULY TO 31 DECEMBER, 1993				
	Prosecutions		**Convictions**	
	Male	**Female**	**Male**	**Female**
Section 6	–	–	–	–
Section 7	5	4	4	3
Section 8	–	28	–	26
Section 9	–	–	–	–
Section 10	–	–	–	–
Section 11	–	–	–	–
Total	**5**	**32**	**4**	**29**
YEAR ENDED 31 DECEMBER, 1994				
	Prosecutions			**Convictions**
	Male	**Female**	**Male**	**Female**
Section 6	–	–	–	–
Section 7	7	9	5	8
Section 8	–	75	–	74
Section 9	–	–	–	–
Section 10	–	–	–	–
Section 11	–	–	–	–
Total	**7**	**84**	**5**	**82**
YEAR ENDED 31 DECEMBER, 1995*				
	Prosecutions		**Convictions**	
Section 6	4		1	
Section 7	19		13	
Section 8	15		12	
Section 10	–		–	
Other offences	18		16	

*** Please note that information as regards gender is not readily available.**

Section 6: Soliciting or importuning for purposes of commission of a sexual offence.
Section 7: Soliciting or importuning for purposes of prostitution.
Section 8: Loitering for purposes of prostitution.
Section 9: Organisation of prostitution.
Section 10: Living on earnings of prostitution.
Section 11: Brothel keeping.

ARTICLE 7

State Parties shall take all appropriate measures to eliminate discrimination against women in the political and public life of the country and, in particular, shall ensure to women, on equal terms with men, the right:

(a) ***to vote in all elections and public referenda and to be eligible for election to all publicly elected bodies;***

(b) ***to participate in the formulation of Government policy and the implementation thereof and to hold public office and perform all public duties at all levels of Government;***

(c) ***to participate in non-governmental organisations and associations concerned with the public and political life of the country.***

The Irish Constitution provides equal rights for men and women to participate in the political and public life of the nation.

Significant progress has been made in recent years in regard to women's access to political and public life. Although, since the foundation of the State there has never been a time when the Dáil (Parliament) was without a woman member, recent elections have seen an increase in women's representation.

The election of Ireland's first woman President in 1990 was a major milestone in achieving women's full integration into political and public life.

The number of successful women candidates in the 1992 Dáil General Election increased significantly, from 7.8% of successful candidates in 1989 to 12% of successful candidates in 1992. The representation of women in the Dáil now stands at 13.85%, following the election of three more women in by-elections since 1992. Women represented 23.17% of national candidates in the EU Parliament election in June, 1994 and 26.77% of successful candidates. It is anticipated that these numbers will increase further in future years.

The present Government includes two women as full Cabinet Ministers (in the Justice and Education portfolios) out of a total of fifteen and three women as Junior Ministers, out of seventeen.

Female membership of the main political parties is not readily available. Fine Gael, the major Government party, estimates that women comprise 30% of the membership, while Fianna Fáil, the largest opposition party, estimates that women comprise 20% of the membership.

Table 7.1 shows the number of female candidates and number successful in General Elections since 1969.

Table 7.1

Women Candidates and Seats Won by Women in Dáil Elections 1969 – 1992

Year	Total No. of Candidates	Women Candidates	Number of Seats	Women Elected	Women Deputies as a % of Total
1969	373	11	144	3	2.1
1973	334	16	144	4	2.8
1977	375	25	148	6	4.1
1981	404	41	166	11	6.6
1982 (Feb)	366	35	166	8	4.8
1982 (Nov)	364	31	166	14	8.4
1987	466	58	166	14	8.4
1989	370	51	166	13	7.8
1992	481	88	166	20	12.0

Source: Department of the Environment, General Election Results

(a) To vote in all elections and public referenda and to be eligible for election to all publicly elected bodies.

Irish women and men are on equal terms regarding the right to vote at all national and local elections and referenda. Similarly, there is no discrimination in relation to the right to stand for such elections or to serve on the relevant public bodies.

Voting in Ireland is by secret ballot and is not compulsory. In the 1992 General Election for the Dáil (House of Representatives) 68% of the electorate cast their vote.

In 1968 Ireland acceded to the United Nations Convention on the Political Rights of Women (1952) which provides that women shall, on equal terms with men and without any discrimination, be entitled to vote in all elections, be eligible for election to all publicly elected bodies established by national law and be entitled to hold public office and to exercise all public functions established by national law. The following tables give an indication of the range and level of participation of women in some sectors of public life.

Table 7.2

Representation of Women on the National Executives of the main Political Parties, February, 1994

	Women as % of Total Membership	% Representation of women on National Executive
Fianna F il	40.0	17.9
Progressive Democrats	45.0	46.6
Labour	33.0	22.0
Fine Gael	30.0	25.0
Democratic Left	37.4	41.0
Green Party	43.0	45.5

Source: Political Parties

Table 7.3

Elected Members of Local Authorities, 1995

Authorities	Number of Authorities	Members	Number of Women	Women as % of total
County Councils	29	753	94	12.5
County Borough Councils	5	130	18	13.8
Borough Corporations	5	60	9	15
Urban District Councils	49	450	71	15.8
Town Commissioners	26	234	49	20.9
Totals	**114**	**1627**	**241**	**14.8**

Source: Department of the Environment

Table 7.4

Number of Women elected and nominated to Seanad Éireann[1], 1969-1992

Year	Taoiseach's Nominees	Panels	Universities	Total Women Members	Women as a % of Total Members
	Number of Seats				
	11	43	6		
1969	1	3	1	5	8
1973	-	3	1	4	7
1977	3	1	2	6	10
1981	1	5	3	9	15
1982 (Feb)	1	6	1	8	13
1982 (Nov)	1	3	2	6	10
1987	-	4	1	5	8
1989	2	3	1	6	10
1992	1	6	1	8	13

1. See Part I, paragraph 2.2.

Table 7.5

Membership of Oireachtas Committees, 1993

Committee	Male	Female	Female % of Total
Joint Committee on Sustainable Development	17	2	10.5
Joint Committee on Small Business and Services	17	2	10.5
Joint Committee on the Family	11	8	42.1
Joint Committee on European Affairs	15	2	11.8
Joint Committee on Foreign Affairs	27	3	10.0
Joint Committee on Women's Rights	5	12	70.6
Joint Committee on Commercial State-Sponsored Bodies	10	1	9.1
Joint Services Committee	17	1	5.6
Joint Committee on Standing Orders	6	0	-
Select Committee on Social Affairs	15	6	28.6
Select Committee on Finance and General Affairs	21	0	-
Select Committee on Enterprise and Economic Strategy	19	2	9.5
Select Committee on Legislation and Security	20	1	4.8
Select Committee on Members' Interests of Seanad Éireann	7	0	-
Select Committee on Members' Interests of Dáil Éireann	5	0	-
Comhchoiste don Ghaeilge (Joint Committee on Irish Language)	15	2	11.8
Standing Joint Committee on Consolidation Bills	6	0	-
Committee of Public Accounts	12	0	-
Seanad Committee on Procedure and Privileges	9	1	10.0
Seanad Committee of Selection	9	1	10.0
Dáil Committee on Procedure and Privileges	16	2	11.1
Dáil Committee of Selection	11	2	15.4
Broadcasting Control Committee	7	1	12.5

(b) ***To participate in the formulation of government policy and the implementation thereof and to hold public office and perform all public functions at all levels of government.***

Participation in Government Policy Formulation and Implementation

Participation in Government policy formulation may take different forms, e.g. input into the policy process such as that provided by lobby, media or pressure groups; being a decision maker in the policy process, for example, as a politician; or being part of the policy-making machinery such as being employed as a Government official or in the wider public service. In each of these aspects, Irish women are guaranteed equal rights with men.

Women are still sparsely represented in all areas of political life, public office and in the higher echelons of the public and civil service in comparison to men. This does not imply, however, that women's interests and special concerns are not observed in the formulation of mainstream Government policy. The Department of Equality and Law Reform, the Joint Parliamentary Committee on Women's Rights, the Employment Equality Agency and the National Women's Council of Ireland are all means by which women's interests are processed and channelled through to Government, thus guaranteeing women not only a direct input to Government policy-making but also a watchdog facility through which progress towards equality can be checked and measured.

Women in Public Office

The number of women who have taken up positions as public representatives at national and local level together with the level of female participation are indicated in the Tables on the previous pages.

Women in the Public Service

The Civil Service

Recruitment to the Civil Service is by open public competition administered by an independent State Commission.

Table 7.6 sets out the gender competition of the main general service grades in the Civil Service during the period 1991-1995, showing 1987 for comparison purposes. Tables 7.7 and 7.8 show, respectively, the proportion of women in general service management grades and the proportion of women in professional, technical and departmental management grades in the Civil Service as at 31 December, 1995.

As of 31 December, 1995, women represented 48% of all staff in the Civil Service. Of those serving at managerial level in the main general service grades, 30% were women. While women are still under-represented at the higher levels in the Civil Service, there has been a considerable increase in the proportion of women in the grades of Principal and higher over the past eight years (Table 7.6 refers). A female Secretary (Director General) was appointed in 1995, the first woman to be appointed to this position since 1959, when the only other female Departmental Secretary to date was appointed.

Table 7.6

Gender Composition of General Service Grades 1987-1995

GRADE	YEAR										NUMBER SERVING ON
	1987		1991		1992		1993		1995[1]		
	Female %	Male %	Female %	Male %	Female %	Male %	Female %	Male %	Female %	Male %	31 DECEMBER 1995[2]
Secretary	0	100	0	100	0	100	0	100	4	96	26
Assistant Secretary	1	99	4	96	5	95	6	94	5	95	94
Principal	5	95	10	90	12	88	12	88	12	88	339
Assistant Principal	23	77	23	77	21	79	22	78	24	76	1007
(Higher Executive Officer (Administrative Officer	34 26	66 74	32 24	68 76	32 20	68 80	36 21	64 79	38 27	62 73	1965) 99)
Executive Officer	44	56	50	50	52	48	55	45	53	47	2514
Staff Officer	67	33	66	34	68	32	72	28	76	24	1180
Clerical Officer	68	32	75	25	77	23	79	21	79	21	4561
Clerical Assistant	83	17	82	18	81	19	81	19	81	19	5028
Paperkeeper	4	96	6	94	4	96	4	96	8	92	184
Services Officer	2	98	4	96	5	95	6	94	6	94	505
Services Attendant	2	98	3	97	0	100	0	100	8	92	65
Cleaner	96	4	94	6	94	6	87	13	88	12	197
											17,764

1 For technical reasons equivalent data is not available for 1994.

2 The numbers quoted here reflect a definition of the grade titles used for purposes of gender balance statistics. This may differ in some respects from that used for purposes of statistics quoted in other contexts. In addition, the numbers reflect the number of people employed, rather than the number of posts which they occupy (i.e. each person jobsharing is counted in his/her own right even though they occupy only half a post).

The current imbalance results from a variety of factors. Although the marriage bar was abolished in 1973, its effects are still felt at the higher levels as it takes time to progress to the highest grades, particularly during a time when staff numbers are under tight control as they have been in the Civil Service for the past ten years. In addition, there are indications that women have a lower participation rate in promotion competitions than men.

The Civil Service is committed to a policy of equality of opportunity for all its staff. To this end, every effort is and has been made to ensure that there are no barriers, hidden or otherwise, preventing women from progressing to the highest positions. The Commentary under Article 5 sets out a number of positive action measures which have been adopted.

Table 7.7

Gender Composition of General Service Management Grades in the Civil Service at 31 December, 1995

Level	Women %	Men &	Number of people serving on 31/12/95[3]
Secretary	4	96	26
Assistant Secretary	5	95	94
Principal	12	88	339
Assistant Principal	24	76	1,007
Higher Executive Officer Administrative Officer	38	62	2,064
			3,530

Table 7.8

Proportion of Women in Professional, Technical and Departmental Management Grades in the Civil Service at 31 December, 1995

Level	Women %	Men &	Number of people serving on 31/12/95[3]
Secretary	0	100	6
Assistant Secretary	11	89	71
Principal	13	87	477
Assistant Principal	16	84	1,257
Higher Executive Officer	25	75	1,748
	20	80	**3,559**

3 See footnote 1 to Table 7.6

4 See footnote 1 to Table 7.6

Local Authorities

The elected local authorities are the county councils (29), county boroughs (5) and borough corporations (5), urban district councils (49) and boards of town commissioners (26). The members of these authorities are elected on a system of proportional representation. Elections are held about every five years. Table 7.3 refers to elected members of local authorities.

The general perception is that the low representation of women in senior grades in the local authority service has not changed much since Ireland's first Report.

The majority of women employed are in the clerical/administrative category, where they account for 62.4% of employees. They accounted for 71.8% of the key recruitment grade of Clerical Officer at end 1992 and 74.4% at end 1994. Women held 59.6% of the posts in the first supervisory grade of Assistant Staff Officer and 43.5% of the posts in the next highest grade of Staff Officer at end 1994.

In the two grades above this level the percentage of posts held by women is lower than that which might statistically be anticipated. However it will be noted that the percentage of women in these grades has increased slightly in the last few years. The relevant statistics are as follows:

	31 December, 1992		31 December, 1993		31 December, 1994	
	Male	Female	Male	Female	Male	Female
Senior Staff Officer (Grade VI)	83%	17%	81.7%	18.3%	79.5%	20.5%
Administrative Officer (Grade VII)	88.5%	11.5%	87.7%	12.3%	87.2%	12.8%

Since 1992 annual staffing returns are being obtained from local authorities on a gender breakdown basis. These will form an important database from which future progress by women in local authority employment can be measured. A survey of female local authority staff in middle management grades has been conducted to establish their views on selection and promotion procedures and their training and development needs. It is hoped that this survey, together with the database referred to above, will provide a valuable input into the design of appropriate measures by local authorities to facilitate the career development of women.

Recruitment of permanent officers to senior management, management and most professional (non-management) positions in local authorities is undertaken by the Local Appointments Commission, an independent statutory body. The Commissioners are committed to a policy of equal opportunity. Selection board members are instructed that it is essential to ensure there is no bias against candidates on grounds of sex or marital status in the selection process, including at interviews, and that assumptions about the suitability of individual officers for certain types of work on grounds of sex or marital status, which could influence the recruitment decision, should not be made.

All other recruitment to local authorities is carried out by each local authority on an individual basis.

Health Services

The Health Act, 1970 provided for the establishment of eight health boards (with local advisory committees), which have been responsible for the administration of the health services in Ireland since 1971.

In 1994 the eight health boards employed over 40,000 people. Women accounted for 76% of the administrative staff (management executive, professional and clerical) with men accounting for 24%. Table 7.9 shows the distribution of women and men at different occupational levels within this category.

Personnel policy for the health service places emphasis on the necessity for each health agency to observe the principle of equality in its employment and personnel practices so as to ensure that all staff, irrespective of gender, have an equal opportunity to develop their potential and to advance on the basis of merit.

A number of positive initiatives have been introduced in the health service to date. These include improvements in recruitment practice and the provision of flexible working arrangements and career breaks. Reference is now made to the employer's commitment to equal opportunities when advertising health service posts.

However, further change will need to take place in a number of areas. The report 'Barriers to Women's Promotion in the Midland and Mid-Western Health Boards' published in 1995 offers a perspective from the viewpoint of female employees which suggests that the main obstacles relate to organisational procedures (training, interviews and promotional paths) and organisational culture. The report provides a valuable input to the review of policy and procedures in all health agencies.

With a view to developing a broadly based approach in the health service to the achievement of equality of opportunity in employment practices, health agencies are currently in the process of reviewing their personnel practices. When completed, the Department of Health and agencies will consider the overall position to see what further action may be required to complement measures already adopted by employers.

Table 7.9

Male/Female Employment Profile of Administrative Staff in Health Boards

	Males	Females
Health Board HQ plus Hospitals	%	%
1. Senior Management/Management	86	14
2. Executive and Administration	53	47
3. Professional	68	32
4. Clerical	11	89
Total	**24**	**76**

Source: 1994 Health Personnel Census.

Medical and Dental

In 1994, 35% of medical and 46% of dental staff were women. (Table 7.10 refers.) There is, however, some evidence that a changing pattern is beginning to emerge. Of 38 consultants appointed in Ireland in 1994, 12 (almost 32%) were women, which suggests that the increase in female medical graduates is gradually being reflected in an increase in the number of female consultants being appointed.

Table 7.10

Male/Female Employment Profile of Medical and Dental Staff in Health Boards

	Males	Females
Medical	%	%
1. Consultant	80	20
2. Registrar	74	26
3. House Officer	65	35
4. Intern	47	53
General Practice		
1. General Practitioner	62	38
Public Health		
1. Director of Community Care	69	31
2. Area Medical Officer	11	89
Dental		
1. Supervisory Grades	74	26
2. Basic Grades	50	50

Source: 1994 Health Personnel Census

Equal Opportunity in Health Boards and Local Authorities
Under the terms of the Statement of Equal Opportunity issued to local authorities and health boards in February, 1990, following negotiations involving local authority and health board management and unions and the Departments of Environment and Health, staff are entitled to avail of the existing national schemes of career breaks and job-sharing. This Statement also commits local authorities and health boards to treat and develop all their employees equally and covers matters such as recruitment, selection, training and development and dealing with harassment.

STATE BOARDS AND COMPANIES

State Boards constitute an important area of public authority and policy-making. Appointments to State Boards are usually made by the Government Minister with appropriate authority in the area. Overall, approximately half of State Board appointments are made directly by the Minister concerned or by the Government while the balance are elected members or are appointed on the nomination of the social partners or other relevant interest groups. In February, 1992 women comprised only 17% of the directly appointed membership of State Boards. Representation of women among nominated members was even lower.

In March, 1993 the Government to set the objective of achieving gender balance in direct appointments to State Boards, with a minimum target of 40% representation of women and men.

Nominating bodies have been asked to comply with the Government's target but in many cases that level of compliance has not yet been achieved. Pressure is being maintained and appointing bodies are being told when making nominations, particularly when more than one appointment is concerned, that they should comply with the standard set by the Government.

Table 7.11 sets out the membership of State boards at 1 December, 1996.

Table 7.11

Composition of State Boards as at 1 December, 1996

Department Responsible	Total Serving Membership	Women	% of Total	Serving Ministerial/ Governmental Nominees	Women	% of Total	Chair		% of Total
							Male	Female	
Agriculture, Food and Forestry	91	25	27.5	62	21	33.9	10	0	0
Arts, Culture and the Gaeltacht	217	81	37.3	145	59	40.7	12	5	29.4
Defence	63	19	30.2	40	13	32.5	2	0	0
Education	486	147	30.2	126	47	37.3	21	4	16
Enterprise and Employment	664	164	24.7	100	33	33	37	9	19.6
Environment	181	58	32	116	43	37.1	13	4	23.5
Equality and Law Reform	24	16	66.7	17	10	58.8	0	2	100
Finance	34	7	20.6	22	5	22.7	3	1	25
Foreign Affairs	73	30	41.1	73	30	41.1	4	1	20
Health	659	181	27.5	275	105	38.2	29	6	17.1
Justice	287	90	31.4	241	85	35.3	22	6	21.4
Office of the Tánaiste	48	24	50	6	4	66.7	1	2	66.7
Marine	576	33	5.7	183	23	12.6	47	1	2.1
Social Welfare	84	45	53.6	63	36	57.1	2	3	60
Taoiseach	62	21	33.9	9	5	55.6	4	0	0
Tourism and Trade	37	13	35.1	34	12	35.3	3	0	0
Transport, Energy and Communications	124	16	12.9	95	16	16.8	11	1	8.3
Total	**3710**	**970**	**26.1**	**1607**	**547**	**34**	**221**	**45**	**16.9**

A survey of equal opportunities undertaken by the Department of Labour in 1991 found that State-sponsored bodies employed 81% men, which reflects the pattern of employment elsewhere in Ireland and the EU.

Distribution of women and men in State sponsored bodies in 1990, by job category was as set out in Table 7.12.

Table 7.12

Category	Female	Male	Recruitment 1990	
			Female	Male
	%	%	%	%
Senior Management	2	98	11	89
Management/Professional	6	94	40	60
Executive/Administrative	28	72	45	55
Professional (non-Management)	10	90	28	72
Technical	13	87	40	60
Clerical	61	39	79	21
Skilled/semi-Skilled/Manual	10	90	13	87

The low level of recruitment to State and Semi-State bodies over the last number of years is a constraint on progress towards a more balanced ratio of female/male employees.

Equal opportunities initiatives in State-sponsored bodies include the provision of crèche facilities, flexible working arrangements, job-sharing and career breaks, adoption of equal opportunities policies, appointment of Equal Opportunities Officers, the provision of special training for female staff and the establishment of structures to examine existing equal opportunities practices and to make recommendations for action.

THE JUDICIARY

The position in relation to women in the judiciary at August, 1996 was as follows:

Table 7.13

Women in the Judiciary, August, 1996

	Total number of Judges	Number of Women	Number of Women	% Female
Supreme Court	8	1	7	12.5
High Court	20	3	17	15.0
Circuit Court	24 (1 vacancy)	2	22	8.3
District Court	46	7	39	15.2

Within the legal profession 24.6% of all barristers were women in 1993 compared to 20.3% in 1986. In relation to Solicitors, 35% of solicitors registered with the Law Society of Ireland in August 1995 were women (Women in the Labour Force, EEA 1995).

SECURITY SERVICES

Women made up 8.5% of the Garda Síochána (police force) in July, 1996 and within the prison service, women represented 10% of total staff.

A Working Party was established in 1991 comprising representatives from all grades within the force to examine equal opportunities within the Garda Síochána. Twenty one recommendations on policy were drawn up. It was decided to run seminars for women only. A Steering Committee was established and personnel were sent on training courses to act as facilitators.

Women members have obtained promotion at a younger age than men. The average age of women promoted to Inspector is 34 compared to 42 for men. In the grade of sergeant the average age of women promoted is 32 compared to 35 for men. Seventy eight per cent of female officers are on operational duties. Female officers are often detailed to deal with rape and incest cases. Training is given and counselling is available to officers who are effected by the trauma of such cases.

The Equal Opportunities Policy and Guidelines for the Civil Service apply to the Prison Service.

The Commentary under Article 11 refers to the position of women in the Defence Forces.

(c) ***To participate in non-governmental organisations and associations concerned with the public and political life of the country.***

There are no legal obstacles to the participation of women in non-governmental organisations and associations concerned with public and political life.

Commentary on Article 7(a) gives an indication of the role of women in public and political life. The National Women's Council of Ireland is referred to in Part 1, paragraph 4.8. Women have played an important role in organisations lobbying for significant legislative reforms which have taken place over the last number of years.

The Women's Political Association works to encourage women to join political parties, to seek officer posts in political parties and to go forward for election. It also promotes female election candidates across all political parties and encourages women to use their vote.

It is open to women to participate in other key non-governmental organisations such as employer and farming bodies and trade unions. While their participation has been limited, it is increasing. However, the division of labour within society has influenced the role played by women in these organisations.

The Irish Congress of Trade Unions has promoted the involvement of women in trade unions, with seats reserved for women on the National Executive, a Women's Committee and biennial women's conference.

ARTICLE 8

States Parties shall take all appropriate measures to ensure to women, on equal terms with men and without any discrimination, the opportunity to represent their Governments at the international level and to participate in the work of international organisations.

In the Department of Foreign Affairs, women occupy 20.1% of the posts from the level of Third Secretary – the key graduate grade for entry to the higher ranks of the Diplomatic Service – upwards, and a breakdown by grade is given in the table under. The Government's equal opportunity policy for the civil service, including appropriate monitoring machinery, is intended to ensure that the prospects of women reaching the higher grades will be enhanced.

Diplomatic staff in the Department of Foreign Affairs (January, 1996)

Grade	Total Posts	Male	Female	% Female
Ambassador Grade I	2	2	—	—
Second Secretary	1	1	—	—
Ambassador Grade II (Deputy Secretary)	6	6	—	—
Minister Plenipotentiary (Assistant Secretary)	36	30	6	16.7
Counsellor	47	40	7	14.9
First Secretary	108	87	21	19.5
Third Secretary	64	45	19	29.7
Totals	**267**	**215**	**52**	**19.5**

Opportunities for women to represent their Government at the international level are not confined to working in the Diplomatic Service. As a member of such international organisations as the United Nations, the European Union, the Council of Europe and the Organisation for Economic Co-Operation and Development, Ireland is called upon to attend a large range of meetings within these fora. No statistics are kept as to the breakdown by sex of civil servants representing Ireland at such meetings, but at all times the overriding consideration in nominating officers to attend is the competence of the officers concerned and their familiarity with the subject matter of the meeting. There is no discrimination on grounds of sex involved in this process and many Irish women represent their country at international meetings in the fora mentioned above.

As regards participation in the work of international organisations, vacancies advertised in those organisations are circulated to all Irish civil servants and every support and assistance is given to intending applicants – regardless of sex – in the preparation of their applications.

The main international organisations in which Irish citizens participate are the European Union and the United Nations. Set out below is a breakdown of the representation of women and men in the administrative grades (or their professional equivalents) in the two organisations at the end of 1993.

Institutions of the European Union

Total Irish representation:	308	
Number of women: A and B grades (administrative/executive)	77	(25%)

UN Institutions (includes Irish representatives working in UN secretariat and agencies based in New York, Geneva and Vienna)

Total Irish representation:	53	
Number of women:	13	(24.5%)

Article 9

1. ***States Parties shall grant women equal rights with men to acquire, change or retain their nationality. They shall ensure in particular that neither marriage to an alien nor change of nationality by the husband during marriage shall automatically change the nationality of the wife, render her stateless or force upon her the nationality of the husband.***

2. ***States Parties shall grant women equal rights with men with respect to the nationality of their children.***

Under provisions of the Irish Nationality and Citizenship Acts, 1956 and 1986, no differentiation is made between the sexes insofar as the acquisition of Irish citizenship is concerned.

Under the Irish Nationality and Citizenship Act, 1986 both the foreign husbands and foreign wives of Irish citizens are entitled to Irish citizenship on the lodgement of a declaration accepting Irish citizenship as post-nuptial citizenship provided that:

(a) the marriage is subsisting at the date of lodgement of the declaration; and

(b) the couple are living together as husband and wife and the spouse who is an Irish citizen submits an affidavit to that effect when the declaration is being lodged.

Under Irish law there is no obligation on citizens to change nationality upon marriage to a non-national. Similarly, change of nationality by either spouse during marriage does not automatically change the nationality of the other spouse, render him/her stateless or force upon him/her the nationality of the other spouse. Furthermore, under Irish law the holding of dual nationality is permitted.

The Irish Nationality and Citizenship Acts, 1956 and 1986 grant women equal rights with men with respect to the nationality of their children.

ARTICLE 10

State Parties shall take all appropriate measures to eliminate discrimination against women in order to ensure to them equal rights with men in the field of education and in particular to ensure, on a basis of equality of men and women:

(a) *the same conditions for career and vocational guidance, for access to studies and for the achievement of diplomas in educational establishments of all categories in rural as well as in urban areas; this equality shall be ensured in pre-school, general, technical, professional and higher technical education, as well as in all types of vocational training;*

(b) *access to the same curricula, the same examinations, teaching staff with qualifications of the same standard and school premises and equipment of the same quality;*

(c) *the elimination of any stereotyped concept of the roles of men and women at all levels and in all forms of education by encouraging co-education and other types of education which will help to achieve this aim and, in particular, by the revision of text books and school programmes and the adaptation of teaching methods;*

(d) *the same opportunities to benefit from scholarships and other study grants;*

(e) *the same opportunities for access to programmes of continuing education, including adult and functional literacy programmes, particularly those aimed at reducing, at the earliest possible time, any gap in education existing between men and women;*

(f) *the reduction of female student drop-out rates and the organisation of programmes for girls and women who have left school prematurely;*

(g) *the same opportunities to participate actively in sports and physical education;*

(h) *access to specific educational information to help to ensure the health and well-being of families, including information and advice on family planning.*

For many years, successive Irish Governments have pursued a policy of equality of educational opportunity for all. Free primary and second level education is available to all and university fees are being abolished on a phased basis over the period 1995/97.

The Government accept that the educational system plays a vital role in the formation of attitudes in society and largely determines the future choice of career and earnings potential for students. The Government also accept that there are inadequacies in the current legislation governing education in Ireland which have been the subject of debate over many years.

While existing inadequacies have not impeded progress and developments in education the Government are committed to reforms which make a case for the status, role and rights of the various participants in education to be defined in legislation.

It is the policy of the Department of Education to take positive action to promote gender equality in education. A Working Group, established within the Department in 1983 and chaired by an Assistant Secretary, promotes, co-ordinates and monitors activities relating to equality issues. In the period since 1986 the Department and its agencies have initiated a wide range of activities, including intervention projects, action research and the production and dissemination of promotional literature.

In 1990 the Minister for Education launched the Department's Policy Document "Department of Education – Gender Equality". This document is an explicit statement of the Department's policy for the promotion of gender equality in education and the elimination of sexism and sex-stereotyping. The areas which the document highlights for monitoring and action are administration, employment, curriculum, initial and in-service training, inspection and management.

The Higher Education Authority (HEA) is a statutory body which has advisory and other functions in relation to higher education. Its functions include funding of universities and designated institutions of higher education and the development of higher education generally to meet the needs of the community. The Higher Education Authority Act assigns to the HEA the general function of promoting the attainment of equal opportunities in higher education.

In 1992 the **Green Paper on Education** was published. It set out the following programme to promote gender equality in education:

- A review of all teaching material in use in schools will be undertaken on a regular basis and action will be taken to ensure that unsuitable material will be withdrawn or adapted. Priority will be given to the review of materials for younger students.
- Second level schools will ensure that their full range of courses is available to students, irrespective of sex. Small and single sex schools will be encouraged to share resources with other schools in order to make this possible.
- Co-education will be encouraged as the norm at both primary and second level.
- The Department of Education will bring about a greater participation of women in management at all levels of the Department, including in the inspectorate.
- All educational institutions, at primary, second and third levels, will develop and publish an active policy to promote greater equality. Their progress in implementing this policy will be reported on in their annual reports.
- All Boards of Management in schools will aim to have a gender balance in their membership. This requirement will also apply to staff selection committees.

In 1995 the White Paper on Education **Charting our Education Future** was published. It further re-affirms the Government's commitment to the promotion of equality throughout the educational system.

The White Paper stresses that the principle of equality is at the heart of the protection of individual rights and the promotion of equality. It states that the education system for the future should have a philosophy that embraces all students, female and male, on a basis of equality. A sustaining philosophy should seek to promote equality of access, participation and benefit for all in accordance with their needs and abilities. Measures to promote equality will include allocating resources to those in greatest need, providing appropriate support systems, and changing the tangible and intangible qualities of the system itself to cater for the diverse educational needs and interests of the population.

Under the programme **A Government of Renewal** agreed in December, 1994, one of the priorities is the promotion of gender equality with particular reference to curriculum and career choice.

Special Measures to Promote Gender Equality

1. Teacher Education Training

Action Research

Action Research on the Integration of Equal Opportunities in the Curriculum of Teacher Education known as TENET (Teacher Education Network) was initiated by the EU Commission in 1988. In 1988/89 the Department of Education, under the auspices of the TENET programme, implemented five Action Research Projects in pre-service and in-service training in association with teacher education agencies and teacher union interests in order to

(i) raise the awareness of teachers concerning gender inequalities in education and in society;

(ii) provide teachers with information and/or practical guidelines.

The results of these projects were disseminated during 1990/91.

TENET Conference

In September, 1991, Ireland hosted an International Conference on TENET which, in line with the aims of TENET itself, sought to heighten awareness of the issues of equality between women and men and the development of practical ways by which equality can be promoted in schools and in classrooms. The findings of the action research and of the workshops and seminars on dissemination held in participating countries were presented at the conference.

In-Career Training

It is a requirement of the Department of Education that all approved summer courses for primary school teachers must cover the topic of gender equality either by way of a specific in-service module or by a permeation approach. This latter approach provides an opportunity for course participants to raise equality issues where they see relevance as well as allowing for discussion. Focused permeation implies some core sessions allied to a wide distribution of references supported by substantial research and not just casual asides.

2. **FUTURES Project**

The Girls into Technology/FUTURES project, co-funded by the Department of Education and the EU, has the specific aim of widening subject choice during Junior Cycle. The project, which includes a pack of teaching materials for different subjects, was first disseminated at the European Conference "Gender across the Curriculum" in 1992, and has been further promoted through a series of regional seminars for post-primary teachers throughout the country. All schools have access to the FUTURES materials and training for teachers involved in their use is available through the network of teachers who have already been trained.

3. **Research Project on Gender Equality in Primary and Post Primary Education (GEAR)**

In 1989 the Department of Education commissioned the Educational Research Centre, St Patrick's College, Dublin, to undertake a research programme aimed at reducing imbalances in the educational experiences of girls and boys in primary schools. A report of the project was published by the Department of Education in 1994 and was circulated to all primary schools as part of a resource pack for teachers to promote equal opportunities for girls and boys in primary education. The resource pack also included a booklet on guidelines for teachers and the report of the working group on the elimination of sexism and sex-stereotyping in textbooks and teaching materials in primary schools.

4. **Promotional Activities**

In 1989 a leaflet entitled **OPTIONS** was produced and sent to all second level schools in the country. This leaflet provided statistics on the take-up by girls of honours mathematics/science subjects at both intermediate and leaving certificate levels, as well as the take-up of non-traditional courses in higher education. It provided information on trends in the labour market and encouraged girls to choose their subject/training/career options very carefully in the light of current trends and to consider a wider range of options both at second-level and in higher education.

In 1990 the Minister for Education launched an **Equality Pack** which was sent to every primary and second-level school in the country. The pack included:

- the booklet entitled, **Department of Education – Gender Equality,** which outlines the equality policy of the Department.
- a copy of an Action Handbook, **How to implement gender equality,** produced by the European Commission. The handbook contains examples and suggestions for action drawn from European experience.
- posters – one for primary schools Develop Them Equally and two for second level schools, Not Me and Go for the Stars.
- leaflets – Could Engineering be for You? and OPTIONS.

A further equality pack issued in 1994 to all primary schools. The pack included recent relevant reports and the results of the GEAR project (see 3 above).

Women in Technology and Science (WITS) provides a role model scheme for second level schools. The Department of Education provided a grant to WITS for the production and publication of a booklet "Suitable Jobs for a Woman". The Department of Education circulated the booklet to all second level schools in 1994.

(a) ***the same conditions for career and vocational guidance, for access to studies and for the achievement of diplomas in educational establishments of all categories in rural as well as in urban areas; this equality shall be ensured in pre-school, general, technical, professional and higher technical education, as well as in all types of vocational training;***

(b) ***access to the same curricula, the same examinations, teaching staff with qualifications of the same standard and school premises and equipment of the same quality.***

There is formal equality between men and women in all sectors and levels of education in Ireland. Specific measures undertaken to achieve de facto equality of opportunity in education are set out above.

In view of recent national and international research which has thrown some doubt on the value of co-education for girls, particularly academically, the Minister for Education commissioned research in 1993, with the following terms of reference:

(a) to determine whether there is a significant difference in girls' attainment levels relative to boys in co-educational schools and also relative to girls and boys in single sex schools;

(b) to determine the causes of such differences, if they are found to exist;

(c) to develop models of good practice to ensure that gender equality for both sexes is provided at school and classroom levels in all schools.

The report "Co-Education and Gender Equality" was published by the Economic and Social Research Institute in 1996. The report proposed an integrated set of policy recommendations aimed at State, local and school level. These are now being considered by the Department of Education.

Table 10.1 shows the number of persons receiving full time education by gender and type of school or college for 1994/95.

Table 10.1

Number of Persons Receiving Full-Time Education by Gender and Type of Institution Attended – 1994-1995

TYPE OF INSTITUTION	MALE	FEMALE	TOTAL
FIRST LEVEL:			
AIDED BY DEPT. OF EDUCATION			
National Schools:	**252,905**	**238,221**	**491,126**
Ordinary Classes	245,847	233,279	479,126
Special Schools+	4,772	2,915	7,687
Special Classes	2,286	2,027	4,313
NON-AIDED PRIMARY SCHOOLS	**4,169**	**3,857**	**8,026**
TOTAL - First Level	**257,074**	**242,078**	**499,152**
of which aided by Dept. of Education	252,905	238,221	491,126
SECOND LEVEL:			
AIDED BY DEPT. OF EDUCATION			
Junior Cycle	**106,410**	**102,507**	**208,917**
Secondary	59,391	71,073	130,464
Community & Comprehensive	17,039	13,335	30,374
Vocational	29,980	18,099	48,079
Senior Cycle (General)	**68,266**	**72,268**	**140,534**
Secondary	41,615	51,408	93,023
Community & Comprehensive	9,772	8,753	18,525
Vocational	16,878	12,100	28,978
Preparatory Colleges	1	7	8
Senior Cycle (Vocational)	**7,469**	**14,349**	**21,818**
Secondary	635	1,368	2,003
Community & Comprehensive	766	1,168	1,934
Vocational	6,068	11,813	17,881
Other Courses	**282**	**406**	**688**
Regional Technical Colleges	282	406	688
Technical Colleges	0	0	0
AIDED BY OTHER DEPARTMENTS (AGRICULTURE/DEFENCE)	**1,371**	**204**	**1,575**
NON AIDED COMMERCIAL	**748**	**1,177**	**1,925**
TOTAL – Second Level	**184,546**	**190,911**	**375,457**
of which aided by Dept. of Education	182,427	189,530	371,957
THIRD LEVEL			
AIDED BY DEPARTMENT OF EDUCATION			
HEA Institutions (Aided)	**24,715**	**28,655**	**53,370**
Teacher Training	**34**	**469**	**503**
Primary	34	268	302
Domestic Science	0	201	201
Technological Colleges	**20,143**	**15,332**	**35,475**
Regional Technical Colleges	14,408	10,544	24,952
Dublin Institute of Technology	5,440	4,401	9,841
Other	295	387	682
Other (National College of Industrial Relations)	**137**	**128**	**265**
AIDED BY OTHER DEPARTMENTS (JUSTICE/DEFENCE)	**666**	**207**	**873**
NON-AIDED	**3,075**	**3,085**	**6,160**
Religious Institutions	694	476	1,170
Royal College of Surgeons in Ireland	536	399	935
Other	1,845	2,210	4,055
TOTAL – THIRD LEVEL	**48,770**	**47,876**	**96,646**
of which aided by Dept of Education	45,029	44,584	89,613
GRAND TOTAL	**490,390**	**480,865**	**971,255**
of which aided by Dept. of Education	480,361	472,335	952,696

Junior Certificate

The Junior Certificate was introduced in 1989, replacing the Intermediate Certificate. The Junior Certificate benefits girls in a number of ways:

(a) the introduction of higher and ordinary levels for all subjects (previously there was one level only) and the introduction also of a foundation level for English, Irish and Mathematics means greater flexibility.

(b) the structure of some of the new syllabi (e.g. Science) in a core plus modular format is a major advance for girls and provides greater flexibility for schools;

(c) the Home Economics syllabus was revised along similar lines with the aim of allowing greater access for boys to this subject;

(d) the provision of access for girls to technology was a central rationale for the Junior Certificate Technology course and many of the schools participating in the pilot stage of the new programme are single sex girls' schools.

The introduction of Civic, Social and Political Education to the curriculum is designed to ensure that, on completion of the junior cycle, all students, in accordance with their abilities and aptitudes, will have achieved or experienced an understanding and appreciation of the central concepts of citizenship.

Leaving Certificate

Table 10.2 provides details of the numbers taking selected subjects at the Leaving Certificate examination, 1994.

There has been an increase in the number of mixed schools offering Building Construction, Engineering and Technical Drawing to both sexes. The number of boys taking Home Economics has increased significantly as has the number of girls studying Mathematics and Physics at the higher levels. The new range of senior cycle courses being offered in schools from September, 1995 has, as a central aim, the elimination of stereotyping in relation to subject choice.

Table 10.2

Number of boys and girls taking selected subjects at Leaving Certificate examination, 1994

Subject	Higher Level		Ordinary Level	
	Female (%)	**Male (%)**	**Female (%)**	**Male (%)**
Irish	9,010 (64.0)	5,071 (36.0)	18,610 (49.9)	18,696 (50.1)
English	16,928 (56.6)	12,957 (43.4)	13,035 (45.8)	15,420 (54.2)
Mathematics	3,281 (40.1)	4,902 (59.9)	23,185 (53.2)	20,379 (46.8)
Applied Mathematics	127 (11.9)	941 (88.1)	28 (12.0)	206 (88.0)
Physics	2,251 (30.2)	5,210 (69.8)	520 (13.8)	3,252 (86.2)
Chemistry	3,091 (49.5)	3,159 (50.5)	652 (38.3)	1,050 (61.7)
Physics and Chemistry	392 (38.5)	626 (61.5)	82 (13.1)	544 (86.9)
Biology	12,003 (70.2)	5,087 (29.8)	7,118 (60.9)	4,567 (39.1)
Home Economics, Social and Scientific	13,016 (86.0)	2,111 (14.0)	4,131 (77.2)	1,217 (22.8)
Home Economics, General	176 (96.2)	7 (3.8)	214 (88.8)	27 (11.2)
Economics	1,408 (33.7)	2,769 (66.3)	513 (28.4)	1,296 (71.6)
Art	4,136 (63.2)	2,405 (36.8)	2,004 (54.1)	1,701 (45.9)
Engineering	80 (2.5)	3,153 (97.5)	96 (4.7)	1,942 (95.3)
Technical Drawing	149 (4.2)	3,404 (95.8)	165 (3.4)	4,696 (96.6)
Construction Studies	109 (2.5)	4,311 (97.5)	98 (4.2)	2,242 (95.8)

Source: Department of Education Statistical Report, 1993/94.

Guidance Services

The promotional activities and curriculum projects already mentioned are normally channelled to the schools through the guidance teachers. In view of their central role in advising young people on choice of subjects and careers, they have been given priority in all the relevant programmes of in-service training. A substantial increase in the allocation of guidance posts to schools began in 1992. (See also under 10(f)).

(c) ***The elimination of any stereotyped concept of the roles of men and women at all levels and in all forms of education by encouraging co-education and other types of education which will help to achieve this aim and, in particular, by the revision of text books and school programmes and the adaptation of teaching methods.***

Positive action measures undertaken to, inter alia, remove stereotypical concepts of the roles of men and women are outlined above. Commentaries on Articles 10(a) and (b) provide information on co-education in Ireland.

Textbooks and Teaching Materials

A Working Group on the Elimination of Sexism and Sex Stereotyping in Textbooks and Teaching Materials in primary schools was established in 1988. The Group comprised representatives of the Department of Education, school management, teacher and parent interests. In addition to an examination of sexism in textbooks and teaching materials, the Group made a study of the course in conversational Irish and examined the guidelines for publishers which must be followed in order to have a textbook approved for use in primary schools. The report of the Working Group was circulated to all primary schools in 1994 as part of the Resource Pack for Teachers.

At second-level, apart from a small number of prescribed tests, decisions on which books to use are taken at school level. Work on the reform of the syllabi by the National Council for Curriculum and Assessment (NCCA) is ongoing. The NCCA is also engaged in regular consultation with the educational publishers regarding the content of syllabuses and material for inclusion in text books.

Hidden Curriculum

The "Hidden Curriculum" is used to describe certain practices and policies, conscious or unconscious, within schools, which re-inforce stereotyped messages regarding boys' and girls' capabilities or appropriate behaviour. The Department of Education, the Irish National Teachers Organisation (INTO), and the Employment Equality Agency have been active in highlighting and challenging this "hidden curriculum". INTO has produced a leaflet for teachers on avoidance of stereotypical behaviour.

School Principal Appointments

There is concern regarding the gender imbalance in relation to school principal appointments. These appointments are a function of individual school management boards.

At primary level 75% of all teachers are women but less than half the principals are women. At second level, 50% of teachers in the community/comprehensive sector are women but only 9% of the principals are women. In secondary schools, 58% of lay teachers are women but only 26% of lay principals are women.

This is an issue of on-going concern to all involved in the provision of education.

Intervention Projects in Physics and Chemistry

A scheme of intervention projects in Physics and Chemistry was established by the Department of Education in 1985. The projects are designed to encourage more girls in the senior cycle of second-level schools to study these subjects.

The projects are implemented through the assignment of an experienced visiting teacher to selected project schools to assist in establishing Physics and/or Chemistry as a subject in the school and to foster an appreciation of these subjects as an integral part of a modern curriculum.

In addition to expanding the curriculum of the project schools, the visiting teachers provide a service to other girls' and co-educational schools in the region.

Each of the projects is closely monitored by the Department of Education's Science Inspectorate. A detailed independent evaluation of the scheme has been carried out. Among the principal findings the evaluators noted that projects had been very successful in promoting Physics and Chemistry in girls' schools which had not previously included these subjects on the curriculum.

A survey of girls from project schools found that over one third of them were working or studying in Science/Engineering-related areas.

The current phase of the Equality Programme is known as the Resources for Equality in the Physical Sciences (REPS) Project. This phase focuses on the provision of resources for teachers, with a particular emphasis on gender equality issues.

(d) ***the same opportunities to benefit from scholarships and other study grants;***

(e) ***the same opportunities for access to programmes of continuing education, including adult and functional literacy programmes, particularly those aimed at reducing, at the earliest possible time, any gap in education existing between men and women.***

There is no discrimination between men and women in access to continuing education, including adult second-chance educational literacy programmes.

The Vocational Education Committees (VECs: these are statutory committees of county councils and certain other local authorities which provide and manage vocational schools and provide vocational and continuation education for their areas) have a statutory obligation to provide adult education. This is fulfilled through running evening classes and, increasingly, day-time classes, for adults.

A Further Education Authority is to be established to provide a coherent national developmental framework appropriate to the importance of vocational education and training outside the third-level sector and adult and continuing education. One of its principal functions will be to ensure a balance of level, type, and variety of programmes to meet student and community needs, including the appropriate location of courses.

The Vocational Training Opportunity Scheme (VTOS)

This is a form of second-chance education for adults aged twenty-one years or over, who have been unemployed for at least six months. Recipients of Lone Parent's Allowance for at least six months are also eligible. Participants get a weekly allowance at the same rate as their unemployment payments and do not lose any secondary benefits (e.g. free medical care, fuel and rent allowances, Christmas bonus) to which they are entitled. Lone Parents continue to be paid Lone Parents Allowance and also retain any extra benefits which may be payable. In addition, a lunch allowance is payable, and in some cases a travel allowance.

Approximately 50% of participants are women, which exceeds the proportion of women registered as unemployed.

Second Level Certificate Courses

Unemployed persons and lone parents can attend second level education at any community, comprehensive, second level or vocational school while continuing to receive their unemployment/lone parent payments. The course of study must be full-time and it must lead to a recognised certificate such as the Junior Certificate, Leaving Certificate or a City and Guilds qualification. Participants must be aged twenty-one or over and have been getting an unemployment or lone parents payment for at least 6 months. Secondary benefits are also retained.

Third Level Allowance

This scheme is in operation for unemployed people and lone parents wishing to pursue a course at third level. They may attend a full-time under-graduate third level course at any third level institution. Participants should be aged twenty-one or over and have been getting an unemployment or lone parent payment for at least six months. Participants continue to receive their Unemployment Benefit/Assistance or lone parent payment throughout the course. Secondary benefits are also retained.

New Opportunities for Women (NOW)

The Regional Technical Colleges have established an equality network under the current round of NOW (See Article 4). This Network, which comprises six RTCs, will undertake actions which focus on gender equality within the RTC colleges and in addition there will be a focus on promoting equality of access and equality of outcomes for women across the broad range of courses on offer.

Other Educational Opportunities

There has been a growth of self-help initiatives for and by women at community level. These groups have been instrumental in facilitating the participation of women in education and encouraging the development of marketable skills. Some of these groups receive funding through the VECs, the Department of Social Welfare and/or health boards, and are assisted by Adult Education Officers in the VECs.

Return to Work courses are run by FÁS – the National Training Authority – to provide opportunities for women interested in joining or returning to the workforce. Women are encouraged to use this programme as a form of preparatory training with a view to undertaking further training.

The European Action Programme for the Vocational Training of Young People and their preparation for Adult and Working Life, known as PETRA, was set up by a Decision of the Council of the European Community in December, 1987. The Irish PETRA Programme is operated under the auspices of the Departments of Education and Enterprise and Employment. Actions to re-inforce girls' access to vocational training in industrial, technical and scientific fields were among the priorities defined in the Council's Decision. In Ireland a number of projects are operating under the PETRA Programme. These projects, which are managed by voluntary or statutory agencies at selected locations throughout the country, are co-ordinated by LEARGAS, the Exchange Bureau. Examples of current projects include:

- Young Women's Career Initiative: designed to offer young women the opportunity to undertake some non-traditional activities;
- Introduction of Non-Traditional Training for Young Women: a training initiative which aims to encourage girls into apprenticeships and other technical training through a pre-apprenticeship course;
- Special Youth and Community Based Projects: these projects aim to develop programmes to address the needs of disadvantaged young people and are directed at personal, community and local development. Programmes for women, as part of the target group, include pre-vocational education and personal development programmes for young single mothers, personal and skills development for young traveller women and personal development programmes for teenage girls.

The women's and men's grant schemes operated by the Department of Social Welfare provide grants to locally-based women's and men's groups involved in programmes of self-help and personal/skills development.

A scheme of grants for lone parents to assist them return to work or take up second chance education opportunities is also in operation. Grants may be made to lone parents support and self-help groups and other groups who work with lone parents. This scheme is of particular benefit to women.

Participation in Higher Education[1]

The distribution of entrants by gender and college type in 1992 is shown in Table 10.3. Overall males constituted a slight majority (51%) of new entrants. While it remains anomalous that females still constitute a slight minority given their higher participation rates in senior cycle of the second level sector (52% of Leaving Certificate candidates were female in 1992) their rate of admission has been rising at a faster rate than that of males. In 1980, 46% of new entrants were females compared to 48% in 1986 and 49% in 1992.

The gender distribution of new entrants is related to the structure of the higher education system. Females constitute a majority (53%) of entrants to the university sector and a huge preponderance (90%) of entrants into the colleges of education. In contrast, they form a smaller percentage (43%) of entrants into the technological sector.

1 *Access to College: Patterns of Continuity and Change*, Professor Patrick Clancy, published by HEA.

Field of Study

The pattern of admission by field of study is strongly differentiated by gender. This differentiation is elaborated in Table 10.4. While females constituted slightly less than half (49%) of all entrants, they formed a large majority of entrants into Education (81%), Hotel, Catering and Tourism (73%) and Social Science (72%). They were also in the majority in six other fields of study: Humanities (63%), Art and Design (61%), Medical Sciences (60%), Combined studies (55%), Commerce (53%), Law (53%), and Science (53%). In contrast, females constituted only 17% of entrants to Technology, which continues to be the most sex-typed field of study. Females were also slightly under-represented (47%) in Agriculture.

The distribution of new entrants by field of study and gender in the **HEA designated colleges** is also highly differentiated by gender as shown in Table 10.5. Social Science, Equestrian Studies, Art and Design, European Studies, Communications and Information Studies and Arts attracted a disproportionate number of female students. In contrast, Engineering, Agricultural Science, and Forestry and Architecture attracted a disproportionate number of male students. Science, Commerce, Law and Dentistry reflect greater gender balance in recruitment with females forming a slight majority in all of these except Commerce. There has been some increase in female representation in what have been traditionally male dominated disciplines. For example, there has been an increase in the representation of females in Agricultural Science and Forestry from 20% in 1986 to 39% in 1992, and in Veterinary Medicine from 34% to 44%.

The distribution of new entrants by field of study and gender in the **non-HEA designated colleges**[2] is also highly differentiated by gender as shown in Table 10.6. For males, General Engineering is the field of study which attracted the largest percentage (36%) of new entrants. In contrast, less than 5% of females entered this field. Business, Administrative and Secretarial Studies attracted the largest percentage, more than 40%, of female students, although in common with Science and Computer Science this field of study is not highly differentiated by gender. The pattern of gender differentiation has not altered significantly since 1986. However, although the overall representation of females in the non-HEA designated sector has declined by two percentage points, their representation in the two most male dominated fields of study has increased by three percentage points in each case.

2 i.e. Regional Technical Colleges, Dublin Institute of Technology.

Table 10.3

Distribution of New Entrants to Higher Education in 1992 by Gender and College Type

COLLEGE TYPE	Male		Female		Total	
	N	%	N	%	N	%
University Sector	5,504	46.8	6,253	53.2	11,757	100
Dublin Institute of Technology	1,601	55.6	1,281	44.4	2,882	100
Regional Technical Colleges	5,163	57.6	3,795	42.4	8,958	100
Colleges of Education	42	9.8	387	90.2	429	100
Other Colleges	611	51.2	582	48.8	1,193	100
TOTAL all Colleges	**12,921**	**51.2**	**12,298**	**48.8**	**25,219**	**100**

Table 10.4

Field of Study of all new Entrants to Higher Education in 1992 and Representation of Females in each Field of Study

FIELD OF STUDY	Male	Female	Total		Representation of Females
	%	%	No.	%	%
Humanities	13.2	24.0	4,638	18.5	63.4
Art and Design	2.6	4.2	847	3.4	60.7
Science	14.0	16.4	3,817	15.2	52.6
Agriculture	1.7	1.6	417	1.7	46.8
Technology	37.6	8.3	5,856	23.3	17.3
Medical Sciences	2.4	3.8	780	3.1	59.9
Education	0.8	3.6	541	2.2	81.0
Law	1.9	2.2	512	2.0	52.9
Social Science	1.6	4.3	728	2.9	72.1
Commerce	22.0	26.6	6,090	24.2	53.4
Hotel Catering & Tourism	1.4	4.0	667	2.7	72.9
Combined Studies	0.8	1.1	241	1.0	55.2
TOTAL %	**100**	**100**	—	**100**	**48.7**
TOTAL No.	**12,888**	**12,246**	**25,134**	—	—

Table 10.5

Distribution of entrants to HEA designated colleges by field of study and gender and representation of females in each field of study, 1992

FIELD OF STUDY	Male	Female	Total		Representation of Females
	%	%	No.	%	%
Arts	27.3	40.0	3,970	34.0	62.4
Education	1.1	0.8	112	1.0	45.5
Art and Design	0.7	1.6	141	1.2	70.9
Social Science	0.5	3.5	244	2.1	88.5
Economics and Social Studies	2.3	1.4	212	1.8	40.1
European Studies	1.9	3.7	336	2.9	68.8
Communication and Information Studies	0.8	3.0	226	1.9	81.0
Commerce	16.3	11.8	1,627	13.9	45.1
Law	2.5	2.5	294	2.5	53.4
Science	17.0	15.5	1,896	16.2	50.8
Engineering	17.8	3.6	1,192	10.2	18.5
Architecture	0.6	0.3	54	0.5	38.9
Medicine	4.8	6.2	648	5.6	59.1
Dentistry	0.6	0.9	87	0.7	63.2
Veterinary Medicine	0.7	0.5	66	0.6	43.9
Agricultural Science and Forestry	2.0	1.1	181	1.6	38.7
Food Science and Technology	0.8	1.1	114	1.0	59.6
Equestrian	0.1	0.3	29	0.2	72.4
Combined Studies	2.0	2.1	241	1.2	55.2
TOTAL	**5,473**	**6,197**	**11,670**	-	**53.1**

Table 10.6

Distribution of entrants to non-HEA designated colleges by field of study and gender, and representation of females in each field of study, 1992

FIELD OF STUDY	Male	Female	Total		Representation of Females
	%	%	No.	%	%
Construction Studies	9.0	2.2	800	5.9	16.4
General Engineering	36.3	4.6	2,972	22.1	9.4
Science	12.1	17.6	1,965	14.6	54.2
Art and Design	3.9	6.8	706	5.2	58.6
Computer Studies	6.4	6.0	838	6.2	43.4
Business Administration and Secretarial Studies	26.0	40.5	4,379	32.5	55.9
Hotel Catering and Tourism	2.4	8.0	667	5.0	72.9
Education	0.6	6.4	429	3.2	90.2
General Studies	3.2	7.8	780	5.3	66.8
TOTAL	**7,415**	**6,049**	**13,464**	-	**44.9**

Developments in Higher Education Institutions

Measures adopted to promote gender equality vary between third level institutions. Some examples are:

- The establishment of official committees in institutions to monitor and report on the position of women academics.
- Special measures for students in their final year at second-level in relation to entry to courses which have an apparent imbalance in the gender mix of students. These include:
  (i) weekend schools and "open days" to introduce students to Physics and other sciences, Engineering and Technology;
  (ii) a special Mathematics examination to facilitate entry of applicants who may not have had the opportunity to study Higher Mathematics at secondary school;
  (iii) highlighting the achievements of women in Engineering, Mathematics and the Natural Sciences in school liaison programmes.
- Introduction of courses in Women's Studies in the universities.

The Higher Education Authority is to be reconstituted with a wider remit. Among other things, it will be responsible for monitoring gender equality policies in third-level institutions and for providing appropriate support at national level.

All the institutions under its aegis will be asked to develop and publish policies to promote gender equality. These will include:

- policies for the promotion of equal opportunities and associated action programmes, including procedures for preventing the sexual harassment of students and employees;

- strategies to encourage increased participation by women students in faculties and courses of study in which they have been traditionally under-represented, including liaison with second-level schools and the preparation and distribution of suitable promotional materials;

- appropriate gender balance on all staff selection boards;

- encouraging and facilitating women to apply for senior academic and administrative positions;

- the putting in place of arrangements to assist students with young children.

The Higher Education Authority, with the co-operation of University College Cork, is funding the post of Organiser for the National Forum on Equality of Opportunity at Third-Level. The tasks of the post holder will include the establishment of a national network for sharing information and ideas on equality-related issues and the development of a data base in this area.

(f) ***the reduction of female student drop-out rates and the organisation of programmes for girls and women who have left school prematurely.***

The commentary on Article 10(e) refers to some initiatives for second chance education.

The development of programmes and curricula which are responsive to the wide range of needs of children, and of young people generally, are important in relation to the reduction of female drop out rates.

Work on the development of detailed guidance on particular aspects of the primary school curriculum is at an advanced stage.

At second level Junior Cycle syllabi have been revised; see 10(a) and (b). One of the major principles underlying curriculum change at junior cycle level is that there should be a range of learning options and teaching strategies to allow for active involvement of students. A further principle is that individual schools should have greater freedom in selecting curriculum content in order to meet the individual needs of students and local circumstances.

At Senior Cycle the major objective for this decade is that 90% of students in an age-group should complete Senior Cycle. This will mean making provision for a widening range of abilities and interests, including those for whom the present Leaving Certificate structure is unsuitable. Since September, 1994 pupils may spend up to a maximum of three years in

Senior Cycle, by opting to follow a Transition Year Programme prior to a two-year Leaving Certificate programme. This option provides opportunities for personal and social development.

The overall aim of the Transition Year Programme is education for maturity with emphasis on personal development including social awareness and increased social competence. The element of work experience – an integral part of the programme – affords students the opportunity to experience work of a non-stereotypical nature. The guidelines for the programme emphasise that Civic, Social and Political Education should permeate all aspects of the programme including the "hidden curriculum" and that gender equality should be emphasised throughout.

It is intended that there will be three Leaving Certificate options:

(i) a Leaving Certificate programme offering subjects at two levels, higher and ordinary, with a third, foundation level in Irish and Mathematics;

(ii) a Leaving Certificate Vocational Programme, the most striking feature of which will be a broader and more interdisciplinary approach to the vocational dimension of the programme. The restructuring will ensure optimum access to vocational education for all students, without gender or other biases;

(iii) a Leaving Certificate Applied Programme, a distinct two year programme, designed for those students who do not wish to proceed directly to third level education or for those whose needs, aspirations and aptitudes are not adequately catered for by the other two Leaving Certificate programmes. The LCA is characterised by educational experiences of an active, practical and student centred nature.

Syllabi for the established Leaving Certificate are being revised, on a phased basis, by the National Council for Curriculum and Assessment. Revised syllabi (Higher and Ordinary Levels) in Irish, French, German, Spanish, Italian and Accounting were introduced in September, 1995. Foundation level syllabi are now available in two subjects – Irish and Mathematics – in addition to the ordinary and higher levels.

Special Needs

Schools serving disadvantaged areas have received additional allocation of resources, including teaching resources, to take account of their special circumstances.

Additional posts have been allocated to schools for remedial education and in respect of pupils with mental and other disabilities. The Schools Psychological Service is being expanded at primary sector and should help in the early identification of difficulties which pupils may experience.

Specific initiatives are outlined in the White Paper on Education to tackle education disadvantage throughout a child's schooling. These include initiatives such as pre-school intervention, special support for schools in disadvantaged areas, the restructuring of the senior cycle, providing where feasible a comprehensive curriculum for all second-level schools and the removal of selective academic entry tests for schools.

Another important element is the provision of alternative ladders of progression for students through, for example, the certification of vocational education and training programmes, ranging from Youthreach to post-Leaving Certificate course.

The Minister for Education intends to continue and further develop the Home-School Links programme in areas of disadvantage, as resources permit. The programme approaches the prevention of educational disadvantage and parent-school collaboration through a range of initiatives, including local co-ordinators, home visits, additional school facilities, parents' education through courses and classes, and teacher education in relation to partnership.

Aimed at the objective "equality of participation", the Junior Certificate School Programme, is designed to reach out more effectively to a small but important minority of students whose particular needs are not addressed adequately in the present, broadly based Junior Certificate.

The programme will be specifically aimed at:

- students who show clear signs of not coping with the volume and complexity of the present mainstream curriculum;
- students who are underachieving significantly in literacy and numeracy;
- students whose attendance and/or behaviour and attitudinal patterns indicate a marked degree of alienation from school;
- students who have specific disabilities which preclude them from participating in regular courses;
- students whose social and cultural environment does not equip them for the requirements of the normal Junior Certificate programme.

Although these objectives will be specified in a national curriculum framework there will be enough flexibility for schools to accommodate the particular needs and abilities of their own students.

The Junior Certificate School Programme will be introduced on a phased basis in the 1996/97 and subsequent school-years.

Students who do not wish to stay on in second level may avail of the educational opportunities offered by the Youthreach programme. Basic skills training, practical work training and general education are major features of this programme.

Guidance and Counselling

The Guidance and Counselling system at second level has been expanded with the result that almost all pupils now have access to this service. A well developed guidance service in schools is important in encouraging pupils to avail fully of educational opportunities. A particular role of the Guidance Service is to encourage females to avail of a wider range of options in education and employment.

The National Centre for Guidance in Education, established in June, 1995, is a support agency for the Department of Education, educational institutions and guidance practitioners. It is a member of the European Union Network of National Resource Centres for Guidance under the LEONARDO Programme (the current EU Programme for Vocational Training).

The Centre

- assists and enhances the practice of guidance and counselling in education,
- promotes the development of materials and of other resources for guidance,
- supports initiatives in guidance practice and research,
- acts as an information centre on vocational information and guidance provision and practice in other Member States,
- takes part in collaborative projects in the field of guidance with other member States.

(g) the same opportunities to participate actively in sports and physical education.

Implementation of the Government's policy on sport is a function of the Department of Education. It is the Department's policy to avoid bias between the sexes in the promotion of sport and, where deemed necessary, to discriminate positively in favour of women's participation. In recent years there has been a dramatic increase in the number of women involved in sport at competitive, administrative and fun levels.

At the competitive level sport is organised through the national governing bodies of sport. Seventy-one governing bodies are grant-aided by the Department of Education towards the cost of administration, coaching, equipment, international competition and special measures designed to increase participation and improve standards. Apart from a very small number of sports which are played exclusively by men or women, these organisations cater equally for men and women.

Since the 1982 campaign to promote greater involvement of women in sport, Cospóir, the National Sports Council and the Sport Section of the Department of Education have attempted to give above average increases in annual grant-aid to women's organisations to encourage them to promote greater participation and to take account of their difficulties in securing sponsorship.

In 1991 the Government directed that public funds should not be allocated to private clubs which operate discriminatory policies which deprive women of the right to apply for full membership.

A new Sports Council was appointed in 9 July, 1996. A Committee for Women in Sport will be established under the auspices of the new Council. This Committee will be representative of many interests and will promote the development of women's sport and the participation of women and girls in sport.

A sports policy group "Strategy for Sport" is currently in operation and is expected to complete its deliberations and produce a plan for sport in all its aspects later this year (1996). This group will address issues relating to women and sport.

A significant factor in the development of sport for women has been the poor coverage given to women's sports by the media, particularly television. The low level of coverage makes these events unattractive to commercial interests and sports organisations generally experience considerable difficulty in securing sponsorship even for major women's events, irrespective of the level and quality of the event.

The situation in this regard, however, is improving with the advent of events such as the Women's Mini-Marathon which receives extensive publicity on a weekly basis for approximately three months prior to the event.

(h) access to specific educational information to help to ensure the health and well-being of families, including information and advice on family planning.

The White Paper on Education outlines the role of each school in promoting good health and well-being in its pupils. This will include involvement of parents in the development of school policy for health promotion, co-operation with statutory and voluntary agencies which are concerned with health, safety and the environment, and the development of educational programmes which combat abuse of all kinds and which promote a healthy lifestyle.

Plans are well advanced for the introduction of a programme of Relationships and Sexuality Education into schools. The programme will, inter alia, enable students to understand human physiology with particular reference to the reproductive cycle and human fertility and to value family life and appreciate the responsibilities of parenthood.

In June 1995 the Department of Health launched a Health Promotion Strategy which set explicit goals and targets and a plan of action for the improvement of people's health and quality of life. In working towards the implementation of the Strategy targets the Department of Health will continue to give priority to the promotion of health at local level, in settings such as the workplace, school, health facility and the community. The Health Promotion Unit of the Department of Health makes available all its literature and its videos on request to schools, youth groups, public health nurses and other interested groups.

In formulating and implementing its public health campaigns, the Health Promotion Unit liaises closely with the Directors of Community Care or the Health Education Officers in the eight health boards.

Primary Education

The overall aims of primary education may be stated as

(i) to enable the child to live a full life as a child, and

(ii) to help her/him to avail fully of further education and to go on to live a full and useful life as an adult.

These aims influence and permeate the entire work of primary education.

Specifically, the syllabus for Physical Education includes personal hygiene, nutrition, safety and aspects of health education relating to alcohol, smoking and the use of drugs as well as the health aspects of recreation. Some of these topics are integrated into other subject areas also and Religious Education is concerned with preparation for life.

Health education has not been a separate subject area at primary level but has tended to be viewed as part of Physical Education. The National Council for Curriculum and Assessment has established a committee to advise on the development of a programme of Social, Personal and Health Education in primary schools as part of the review of the primary curriculum which is currently underway. The programme of Relationships and Sexuality Education, mentioned earlier, will be integrated into the Social, Personal and Health Education programme. A programme of substance abuse awareness and prevention will be part of this also.

The Departments of Health and Education have developed a child abuse prevention programme called "Stay Safe" in association with the Eastern Health Board, the National Parent's Association (Primary) and primary school managerial bodies. Following a pilot series in the schools in Dublin in 1989/90 it was implemented in all primary schools in the Eastern Health Board area. A Child Abuse Prevention Programme has been available to all schools in the country since 1992. Regional teams consisting of teachers and social workers liaise with schools and community care staff and child psychiatric services in the delivery of the programme. A survey carried out in early 1995 showed that of a total of 3,310 schools, 3,300 (99.7%) had availed of teacher training and 1,980 (60%) were already teaching the programme. It is believed that the number of schools teaching the programme will rise above 80%.

Second Level

With regard to second level education, all schools aspire to the education of the whole person, which includes taking account of the social, personal, physical and spiritual needs of students as well as intellectual needs. Second level schools make provision for education for life and for matters such as relationships and parenting, in the context of this overall aspiration and mission. Generally, the elements of an education for life programme in post-primary schools are included in subjects such as Science, Home Economics, Religious Education and Civics, as well as within the Pastoral Care Programme of the school. This work is often supported by the Guidance and Counselling Programme of the school.

An increasing number of second level schools are arranging for one class period per week for a topic which may be variously called: Social and Personal Development, Life Skills, Health Education or some other such title.

The Departments of Health and Education support teacher in-service training for programmes of the type mentioned and the development of resource materials in relation to matters such as HIV/AIDS, substance abuse and health education generally. School programmes deal with growth and development, relationships with other people, decision-making and influences on decisions, as well as with issues such as family life, general health matters and specific issues such as smoking, drinking, etc. Parenting is an issue dealt with in many of these programmes.

Civic, Social and Political Education (CSPE) will be introduced as part of the Junior Cycle curriculum in second level schools from September, 1996. It will form part of the core curriculum from September, 1997 onwards. CSPE encourages an awareness of attitudes of intolerance and discrimination in all forms – including attitudes directed against women.

The development of a Relationships and Sexuality Education Programme in the context of a broad Social Personal and Health Education Programme is currently under way. This initiative should make it possible for a large number of schools to treat the broad area of health education in a more comprehensive manner.

The Departments of Health and Education have developed a comprehensive substance abuse prevention programme for second level schools. The programme addresses the areas of identity and self esteem, understanding influences, assertive communication, feelings and decision-making. This programme has been introduced to about fifty per cent of schools (1995) and in-service training and wider dissemination are continuing.

The Health Promoting School Project

The European Network of Health Promoting Schools was established in 1992 by the Council of Europe, the European Commission and the World Health Organisation. Ireland joined this project in Autumn 1992 and in 1993 ten schools, comprising five primary and five post-primary, were designated as Project Schools.

These schools committed themselves to a three year pilot programme to facilitate the development of healthy lifestyles for the total school population by developing supportive environments, conducive to the promotion of health. To put this ideal into practice, schools focus on three important aspects:

(i) a health promoting physical and social environment;

(ii) a social, personal and health education curriculum;

(iii) links with families and the community.

The ten schools involved in the Pilot Phase of the Irish Network of Health Promoting Schools have shown great commitment to implementing the Health Promoting School philosophy.

At primary level, involvement in the Health Promoting School network has led to a higher level of awareness of the importance of a balanced curriculum, an enhancing atmosphere and the need for tolerance. Relationships have improved and there is a greater parental involvement. It has led to greater interaction and understanding between the partners in education and a greater awareness of community resources. It has also enhanced understanding between primary and post-primary schools.

The influence of involvement in the Health Promoting Schools Network at second level has led to improved parent/teacher/student three way communication. Student leadership has developed somewhat and the issue of bullying has been and is being addressed. Attention has been paid to the importance of school ethos and environment; behaviour/discipline structures have improved. Positive feedback is given more frequently and students with difficulty are noticed earlier. Care of the less able is enhanced and there is more extra-curricular participation and acknowledgement of non-academic achievement and effort.

The Irish Network of Health Promoting Schools is managed jointly by the Departments of Education and Health and the Marino Institute of Education. It is planned to expand in 1996 by designating 30 additional schools as members of the European Network of Health Promoting Schools.

Article 11

1. *State Parties shall take all appropriate measures to eliminate discrimination against women in the field of employment in order to ensure, on a basis of equality of men and women, the same rights, in particular:*

   (a) *the right to work as an inalienable right of all human beings;*

   (b) *the right to the same employment opportunities, including the application of the same criteria for selection in matters of employment;*

   (c) *the right to free choice of profession and employment, the right to promotion, job security and all benefits and conditions of service and the right to receive vocational training and retraining, including apprenticeships, advanced vocational training and recurrent training;*

   (d) *the right to equal remuneration, including benefits, and equal treatment in respect of work of equal value, as well as equality of treatment in the evaluation of the quality of work;*

   (e) *the right to social security, particularly in cases of retirement, unemployment, sickness, invalidity and old age and other incapacity to work, as well as the right to paid leave;*

   (f) *the right to protection of health and to safety in working conditions, including the safeguarding of the function of reproduction.*

2. *In order to prevent discrimination against women on the grounds of marriage or maternity and to ensure their effective right to work, State Parties shall take appropriate measures:*

   (a) *to prohibit, subject to the imposition of sanctions, dismissal on the grounds of pregnancy or of maternity leave and discrimination on the basis of marital status;*

   (b) *to introduce maternity leave with pay or with comparable social benefits without loss of former employment, seniority or social allowances;*

   (c) *to encourage the provision of the necessary supporting social services to enable parents to combine family obligations with work responsibilities and participation in public life, in particular through promoting the establishment and development of a network of childcare facilities;*

   (d) *to provide special protection to women during pregnancy in types of work proved to be harmful to them.*

3. ***Protective legislation relating to matters covered in this article shall be reviewed periodically in the light of scientific and technological knowledge and shall be revised, repealed or extended as necessary.***

The Anti-Discrimination (Pay) Act, 1974 and the Employment Equality Act, 1977 prohibit discrimination in employment on the basis of gender.

On acceding to this Convention, Ireland entered the following reservation in relation to Article 11.1:

> Ireland reserves the right to regard the Anti-Discrimination (Pay) Act, 1974 and the Employment Equality Act, 1977 and other measures taken in implementation of the European Economic Community standards concerning employment opportunities and pay as sufficient implementation of Articles 11.1 (b), (c) and (d).

It was considered prudent to enter such a reservation because, while the two Acts quoted above comply with European Community standards, which are recognised internationally as being of the highest level, the 1977 Act does not provide women with a blanket right to the same employment opportunities as men. Accordingly, such exceptions to the rights set out in Articles 11.1 (b), (c) and (d) as are implicit in the Convention will be assessed in Ireland by reference to European legislative exemptions.

Section 12 of the Employment Equality Act, 1977, as amended by the European Communities (Employment Equality) Regulations, 1985, provides that the Act does not apply to (a) employment in the Defence Forces or (b) employment which consists of the performance of services of a personal nature, where the sex of an employee constitutes a determining factor.

Section 17 of the 1977 Act, as amended by the European Communities (Employment Equality) Regulations, 1985, provides that the Act does not apply (a) where the sex of the person is an occupational qualification or (b) to posts in the Garda Siochána (Police Force) and Prison Service on the grounds of privacy and certain specific duties.

With regard to the Defence Forces, the Government is committed to a policy of equal opportunity for women and to the full participation of women in all aspects of Defence Force activity, including operational and ceremonial duties, assignments and promotion.

The current (August, 1996) strength of the Permanent Defence Force is 12,584 made up of 1,527 officers, 5,041 non-commissioned officers (NCOs), 5,948 privates and 68 cadets in training. Included in those figures are 54 female officers, 33 female NCOs, 93 female privates and 6 female cadets (i.e. the total number of female members is less than 1.5%). There are 3,060 (August, 1996) women serving in the FCA (local reserve defence force) which has a total strength of 14,975. Of these 62, or just over 2%, are NCOs, compared to 2,969 male NCOs, i.e. 24.9% of total men. In the 1994 recruitment campaign for the Army the basis of selection was suitability rather than gender. Women were for the first time eligible to compete on the same basis of men, 14% of the applications received were from women and 15% of those enlisted were women.

Women are now eligible to serve in the Army, the Air Corps and the FCA on an equal basis and under the same conditions as those which apply to men. Female personnel undergo the same training and military education as men. It was decided in 1993 that women should be given the same opportunity of serving in all branches of the Naval Service, including sea-going appointments and the first female cadets were appointed to the Naval Service in September 1995.

Female Labour Force Participation

In the area of employment, due, inter alia, to Ireland's demographic structure the most significant statistic impacting on the labour force is the high unemployment rate. However since the enactment of equality legislation in the 1970's the labour force participation rate of married women has increased significantly, from 7.5% in 1971 to 37.3% (including separated women) in 1996. The overall participation rate for women in 1996 was 38.5%.

The following tables provide statistical information on the participation of men and women in the labour force.

Table 11.1

Estimated population aged 15 years and over classified by principal economic status and sex, 1992-1996

PRINCIPAL ECONOMIC STATUS	SEX	1992	1993	1994	1995	1996
		THOUSANDS				
IN THE LABOUR FORCE						
At work	Male	742.2	737.6	753.5	783.5	797.3
	Female	400.6	410.5	428.5	455.4	488.0
	Total	1,142.8	1,148.0	1,182.0	1,239.0	1,285.3
Unemployed, having lost or given up previous job	Male	144.1	149.2	140.7	123.8	117.0
	Female	41.9	45.7	43.6	36.4	40.3
	Total	185.9	194.9	184.3	160.2	157.3
Unemployed, looking for first regular job	Male	19.6	21.0	21.8	18.9	20.7
	Female	11.5	13.8	12.3	11.7	11.9
	Total	31.1	34.7	34.0	30.6	32.6
Total in Labour Force	Male	905.9	907.7	915.9	926.3	935.0
	Female	453.9	470.0	484.4	503.5	540.2
	Total	1,359.8	1,377.7	1,400.4	1,429.8	1,475.2
NOT IN THE LABOUR FORCE						
Student	Male	155.7	165.1	166.1	167.2	176.1
	Female	155.1	161.9	166.2	173.7	181.9
	Total	310.8	326.9	332.3	340.9	358.0
On Home Duties	Male	7.7	9.0	9.4	9.9	8.8
	Female	645.8	627.0	628.7	617.8	573.1
	Total	653.5	636.0	638.1	627.7	581.9
Retired	Male	165.2	168.9	167.4	173.3	177.6
	Female	47.6	56.6	55.3	55.8	74.5
	Total	212.8	225.6	222.7	229.2	252.1
Unable to work due to permanent sickness or disability	Male	47.6	43.0	46.4	43.5	45.4
	Female	21.2	16.1	18.8	18.8	19.1
	Total	68.8	59.1	65.2	62.3	64.5
Other	Male	7.4	11.6	12.7	13.3	11.1
	Female	8.9	16.7	10.4	13.1	14.2
	Total	16.3	28.3	23.1	26.5	25.2
Total not in the Labour Force	Male	383.7	397.6	402.0	407.3	418.9
	Female	878.6	878.2	879.4	879.2	862.7
	Total	1,262.2	1,275.8	1,281.4	1,286.5	1,281.7
POPULATION AGED 15 YEARS AND OVER	Male	1,289.5	1,305.3	1,317.9	1,333.6	1,353.9
	Female	1,332.5	1,348.2	1,363.8	1,382.7	1,402.9
	Total	2,622.0	2,653.5	2,681.7	2,716.3	2,756.9

Note: The Labour Force in these tables comprises persons at work, persons unemployed, having lost or given up previous jobs and those looking for their first regular job. The participation rate is defined as the ratio of persons in the Labour Force to the total population in the relevant age group and marital status cell.

Table 11.2

Female Participation Rates by Marital Status

MARITAL STATUS	1988	1989	1990	1991	1992	1993	1994	1995	1996
	%								
Single	51.4	51.0	51.7	50.0	49.8	49.3	49.2	48.7	49.1
Married	23.1	23.5	25.2	26.9	29.2	30.9	32.4	34.2	36.6
Separated*	37.2	35.3	33.4	38.8	39.9	38.4	40.9	41.3	47.3
Widowed	7.4	7.0	7.0	7.4	7.5	7.3	6.8	6.7	8.1
TOTAL	**31.2**	**31.2**	**32.5**	**32.9**	**34.2**	**34.9**	**35.7**	**36.5**	**38.5**

Table 11.3

Female Participation Rates by Age Group

AGE GROUP	1988	1989	1990	1991	1992	1993	1994	1995	1996
	%								
15 – 19	25.1	23.6	23.6	21.1	19.5	17.1	15.2	15.0	14.6
20 – 24	72.5	73.8	73.1	73.3	69.7	69.2	69.7	68.4	66.6
25 – 34	50.9	52.3	54.8	57.4	60.6	61.8	65.0	66.2	69.1
35 – 44	28.0	29.6	32.4	35.4	37.7	41.1	42.7	46.2	50.6
45 – 54	26.3	25.5	27.8	28.8	31.0	31.9	32.9	34.7	38.7
55 – 59	20.8	19.8	21.8	22.2	22.4	23.3	23.2	23.5	27.9
60 – 64	13.5	13.3	14.6	14.1	13.4	13.6	15.2	14.0	15.9
65 and over	3.5	3.1	3.1	3.0	3.1	2.8	2.1	2.5	2.7
TOTAL	**31.2**	**31.2**	**32.5**	**32.9**	**34.2**	**34.9**	**35.7**	**36.5**	**38.5**

* including divorced

Table 11.4

Labour Force Participation Rates for Married and Separated* Females by Age Group

AGE GROUP	1988	1989	1990	1991	1992	1993	1994	1995	1996
	%								
15 – 19	30.5	28.6	24.0	27.7	28.5	30.6	25.8	23.6	26.2
20 – 24	42.3	41.3	46.9	45.9	46.7	51.5	51.2	55.7	52.4
25 – 34	38.2	39.2	40.8	44.8	48.6	50.0	54.1	54.9	57.9
35 – 44	22.7	23.7	26.7	30.6	33.1	36.2	37.6	41.8	46.4
45 – 54	20.6	20.7	22.0	23.4	26.2	28.1	29.4	31.6	34.7
55 – 59	14.0	13.5	15.6	16.7	17.5	19.3	19.8	19.8	23.6
60 – 64	8.3	7.5	9.0	9.6	8.6	9.7	12.3	11.0	12.6
65 and over	1.9	2.3	2.1	2.1	2.2	2.2	2.0	2.6	2.6
TOTAL	**23.6**	**23.7**	**25.3**	**27.4**	**29.7**	**31.3**	**32.8**	**34.6**	**37.3**

Table 11.5

Labour Force: Participation Rates for Single Females by Age Group

AGE GROUP	1988	1989	1990	1991	1992	1993	1994	1995	1996
	%								
15 – 19	25.0	23.6	23.6	21.6	19.5	17.1	15.2	15.0	14.6
20 – 24	80.0	81.2	77.6	77.4	72.8	71.1	71.5	69.5	67.6
25 – 34	87.6	87.5	88.2	87.0	86.2	85.4	85.8	85.4	85.4
35 – 44	79.4	79.2	81.6	78.4	76.2	80.5	80.9	78.9	80.6
45 – 54	69.2	64.8	69.7	71.9	70.4	66.6	67.3	69.4	74.9
55 – 59	55.4	51.6	56.0	55.6	53.8	51.9	47.9	52.0	60.4
60 – 64	36.4	32.6	36.7	36.2	36.3	35.9	33.0	34.8	36.2
65 and over	8.3	7.4	7.2	6.8	6.9	5.4	4.1	4.7	5.0
TOTAL	**51.1**	**50.5**	**51.0**	**50.0**	**49.8**	**49.3**	**49.2**	**48.7**	**49.1**

* including divorced

Table 11.6

Males: Participation Rate By Marital Status									
%									
MARITAL STATUS	**1988**	**1989**	**1990**	**1991**	**1992**	**1993**	**1994**	**1995**	**1996**
Single	63.4	61.9	61.9	61.1	60.6	60.3	60.2	60.4	59.9
Married	82.1	81.2	81.1	81.0	80.8	79.9	80.2	79.8	79.4
Separated*	77.7	78.0	75.2	75.4	75.9	77.2	78.1	77.7	77.2
Widowed	23.8	22.2	19.2	21.5	21.4	22.8	21.4	23.0	22.5
TOTAL	**72.6**	**71.2**	**70.9**	**71.7**	**70.4**	**69.7**	**69.7**	**69.5**	**69.1**
Males: Participation Rate By Age Group									
%									
AGE GROUP	**1988**	**1989**	**1990**	**1991**	**1992**	**1993**	**1994**	**1995**	**1996**
15 – 19	32.0	30.4	29.2	29.2	26.2	24.0	22.4	22.6	21.8
20 – 24	85.0	82.1	81.5	81.1	78.5	75.6	76.1	77.6	74.5
25 – 34	96.9	96.4	96.2	96.1	95.4	95.1	94.9	95.0	95.1
35 – 44	95.8	95.3	95.8	96.0	95.6	94.9	95.1	94.9	95.3
45 – 54	91.8	90.8	91.3	91.7	91.4	91.0	91.0	90.7	91.1
55 – 59	81.4	79.0	79.5	79.9	77.8	78.3	77.4	78.6	76.0
60 – 64	64.3	60.5	57.4	59.5	58.5	57.5	59.6	58.4	54.6
65 or over	18.0	16.7	16.1	16.1	16.4	15.5	15.6	14.6	14.8
TOTAL	**72.6**	**71.2**	**70.9**	**71.1**	**70.4**	**69.7**	**69.7**	**69.5**	**69.1**

Table 11.7

Female Labour Force Classified by Broad Occupational Group

	1986			1990			1993			1996		
	000	**% of female labour force**	**% of total employed in group**	**000**	**% of female labour force**	**% of total employed in group**	**000**	**% of female labour force**	**% of total employed in group**	**000**	**% of female labour force**	**% of total employed in group**
Agricultural Workers	14.1	4.2	8.3	13.3	3.5	7.9	11.3	2.8	7.8	14.4	2.9	10.3
Producers, Makers and Repairers	39.8	11.7	17.4	39.5	10.6	16.8	39.0	9.5	17.2	44.2	9.1	16.9
Labourers and Unskilled Workers	0.5	0.1	1.3	1.0	0.3	2.7	1.1	0.3	3.8	2.8	0.6	7.2
Transport & Communication Workers	7.8	2.3	10.8	8.0	2.2	11.2	8.8	2.2	11.9	9.0	1.8	11.5
Clerical Workers	92.7	27.3	72.8	103.1	27.7	75.7	109.6	26.7	78.2	125.2	25.7	77.4
Commerce, Insurance and Finance Workers	44.4	13.1	33.7	46.3	12.5	34.6	58.8	14.3	40.1	64.4	13.2	42.7
Service Workers	51.6	15.2	53.8	54.9	14.8	54.9	66.5	16.2	58.0	85.8	17.6	60.9
Professional and Technical Workers	82.3	24.2	49.1	96.8	26.1	51.4	103.7	25.3	50.9	125.5	25.7	53.0
Others	6.4	1.9	12.6	8.7	2.3	15.6	11.3	2.7	17.1	16.7	3.4	22.1
TOTAL	**339.5**	**100**	**31.4**	**371.5**	**100**	**32.9**	**410.2**	**100**	**35.8**	**488.0**	**100**	**38.0**

Source: Labour Force Surveys

(a) ***the right to work as an inalienable right of all human beings.***

The right to work or to earn a livelihood, as a personal right, has been identified in the Irish Courts as existing in the guarantees of Article 40.3.1 of the Irish Constitution which states that the State "guarantees in its laws to respect, and, as far as practicable, by its laws to defend and vindicate the personal rights of the citizen". Article 45.2.1 provides that the State shall, in particular, direct its policy towards securing:

> *That the citizens (all of whom, men and women equally, have the right to an adequate means of livelihood) may through their occupations find the means of making reasonable provision for their domestic needs.*

Ireland's high unemployment rate has already been referred to. The Government are committed to combating unemployment. They agreed a three-year programme with the social partners i.e. employers, workers and farming organisations in 1991, the **Programme for Economic and Social Progress** (PESP) had as its main objectives the continued development of the economy, increasing employment and the reduction of Government debt. A successor to PESP, the **Programme for Competitiveness and Work,** was agreed in February, 1994. The Government's clear objective for the discussions that led to this Programme was to make work the cornerstone of development action for the three years of the programme.

A new national agreement **Partnership 2000, for Inclusion, Employment and Competitiveness** represents a strategic approach to lead the Irish economy and society into the 21st Century. The key objectives of the strategy are the continued development of an efficient modern economy capable of high and sustainable economic and employment growth and operating within the constraints of international competitiveness, ensuring that Irish society becomes more inclusive, that long-term unemployment is substantially reduced and that the benefits of growth are more equally distributed.

The process of negotiation leading to the Programme was wider and more inclusive that previous agreements, involving representatives of voluntary community based organisations, including the National Women's Council of Ireland.

The Government published a **Strategy Paper on the Labour Market** in April, 1996 which adopts the goal over time of full employment. It defines this goal as meaning:

- paid employment is available to all who genuinely seek it;
- paid employment is available to meet individual needs and circumstances;
- no person feels obliged to emigrate to find a job;
- unemployment in general will be transitional rather than long-term.

On foot of this Paper the Government agreed the following fundamental imperatives to guide strategy in the labour market:

(a) maximising employment growth and the incentives to create employment;

(b) reducing the disincentives to accept employment;

(c) improving equity of access to employment and promoting equal opportunities between women and men;

(d) tackling educational disadvantage.

The Government also decided that the priority categories for support in labour market programmes must be the long-term unemployed, people with disabilities, members of the Travelling community, women who suffer particular disadvantage in the labour market and those under 21 without qualifications.

(b) the right to the same employment opportunities, including the application of the same criteria for selection in matters of employment;

(c) the right to free choice of profession and employment, the right to promotion, job security and all benefits and conditions of service and the right to receive vocational training and retraining, including apprenticeships, advanced vocational training and recurrent training.

As already indicated, the Employment Equality Act, 1977 makes it unlawful to discriminate on grounds of sex or marital status in relation to recruitment for employment, conditions of employment, training or in opportunities for promotion. A specific provision of a positive action nature is also included in the Act for the provision of vocational training in cases where a particular sex is under-represented in an area.

While the 1977 Act is aimed primarily at the prevention of discrimination by employers, it also prohibits discrimination by organisations concerned with the provision of training courses as well as placement and guidance services provided by employment agencies.

Grievances under the Anti-Discrimination (Pay) Act, 1974 and the Employment Equality Act, 1977 can be pursued by any person in proceedings before Equality Officers, the Labour Court and, in certain circumstances, the Civil Courts. The Employment Equality Agency (EEA) can assist claimants before the Equality Officers and the Labour Court.

As reported in Ireland's First Report, the EEA published a Code of Practice on Equality of Opportunity in Employment, which was updated in 1991 and again in 1994, in an edition for the vocational education sector. The purpose of the Code is to provide guidelines and advice for employers, workers, trade unions and employment agencies to help them to eliminate unlawful discrimination and to avoid its recurrence.

The Employment Equality Act, 1977 gives the Minister power to repeal or amend, where there is no longer a justification for their inclusion, provisions in protective legislation enacted in the period 1936 to 1965, which have the secondary effect of restricting career opportunities for women.

The Employment Equality Act, 1977 (Employment of Females on Underground Work in Mines) Order, 1989 which came into effect on 19 June, 1991 allows women to work in all occupations, including manual occupations below ground in a mine. Prior to this women could only be employed in non-manual occupations below ground in a mine.

Unfair Dismissals Acts, 1977 to 1995

The Unfair Dismissals Acts, 1977-1995 provide that generally it shall be unfair to dismiss a worker because of her pregnancy or matters connected therewith or because she exercises her rights under the Maternity Protection Act, 1994 or the Adoptive Leave Act, 1995.

Maternity Protection Act, 1994

The purpose of this Act is to provide maternity protection for pregnant workers. See Article 11.2(b).

Part-Time Workers

Regular part-time employment increased from 82,600 to approximately 151,400 workers between 1989 and 1996. Labour Force Survey statistics indicate that over 73% of part-time workers are female. In 1996 approximately 76% of female part-time workers were married, compared to 41% of male part-time workers and 52% of females were aged 25-44.

Following a review of the legal protection available to part-time workers The Worker Protection (Regular Part-time Employees) Act, 1991 was introduced. It extended the scope of other protective legislation to all regular part-time employees. Regular part-time employees are defined as those who have worked at least thirteen weeks for an employer and work a minimum of eight hours per week.

Positive Action in Training

FÁS, the National Training and Employment Authority, has a significant role to play in ensuring that there is equality of opportunity in training.

In 1990, FÁS launched its Positive Action Programme **Women in Focus** with a view to improving women's position in the labour market. The programme has the following objectives:

- to promote the breaking down of the traditional patterns of occupational segregation by encouraging increased female participation in sectors of the labour market traditionally dominated by men;
- to promote the participation of women at all levels in growing, future-oriented sectors of the labour market, including technical and managerial occupations, in order to achieve better use of human resources;
- to promote the upgrading of existing skills levels among women.

In 1986, 34% of all of those completing training were women; this rose to 42.2% in 1995. In addition, 37.7% of the throughput on FÁS employment programmes were women in 1995. Since 1990 FÁS has organised preparatory training courses designed to equip women with the necessary basic skills and experiences to enable them to compete on an equal basis for places on apprenticeship or non-traditional skills training courses.

FÁS is the national body with overall responsibility for the registration of all apprentices in the designated trades over the period of their apprenticeship. Since 1990 there has been a small but gradual increase in the number of women entering into apprenticeship training. In 1993, the new standards-based apprenticeship system was introduced alongside the existing time-served apprenticeship system.

Under the standards-based apprenticeship system FÁS no longer has any direct involvement in the recruitment of apprentices. With this development FÁS ceased to set targets for the intake of women into designated apprenticeships in 1994. However, FÁS has taken and continues to take steps aimed at the promotion of recruitment of women into the designated apprenticeships. These steps include:

- a pre-training programme is being developed for educationally disadvantaged persons and will be implemented later in 1996. Its aim will be to provide real second chance education and training to persons not qualified for entry to FÁS mainline Specific Skills Training courses or for entry to apprenticeship due to lack of opportunity as a result of age, gender or lack of maturity or support while in education. It will address the typical gaps in education experienced by individuals, including women, such as in general science, drawing, maths and exposure to craft-type skills,
- FÁS has continued the provision of a financial incentive to employers, in the form of a bursary, to encourage the recruitment of women apprentices. The bursary has recently been extended to public sector employers so that it now applies to all employers,
- a video and information pack aimed specifically at encouraging women to participate at all levels in the construction industry has been widely distributed in the second level education sector,
- a video, The Real Thing, which promotes the standards-based apprenticeship and careers as craftspersons has also been widely distributed to second level schools and colleges,
- a code of practice has been developed in consultation with the social partners with the objective of eliminating inequality in the recruitment of apprentices and promoting the employment as apprentices of persons who traditionally have been under-represented in apprenticeship, including women. The code has been formally endorsed by the social partners,
- support mechanisms for women in apprenticeship and other non-traditional training courses are provided through the on-the-job monitoring process operated by FÁS services to industry, in respect of the standards-based apprenticeship, and

by way of the FÁS positive action programme for women which is reviewed and re-structured annually.

Return to work courses are aimed at the long-term unemployed and those wishing to return to work after an extended absence from the labour market, particularly women. The programme helps participants to develop the confidence necessary to re-enter the labour force and is also an important bridging programme for progression onto other FÁS programmes. In 1995, 92% of participants who completed such training were women. In addition, 63% of participants who completed Enterprise Training were women and women represented 25% of the throughput on the Enterprise Scheme, which provides advice and income support to unemployed people starting businesses.

Under the Specific Skills Training Programme, FÁS provides childcare training with certification.

The upgrading and development of new skills for women already in employment is a vital part of the overall strategy to improve the position of women in the labour force. A major intervention by FÁS is the Training Support Scheme which, through grant aiding training of existing employees, is designed to increase and improve the competitiveness, quality and productivity of Irish business. In 1995 33% of employees whose training was grant aided were women. In 1995 equal opportunities training initiatives were specifically eligible for support.

CERT, the state tourism training agency, implements a policy to ensure equality of access to all tourism training programmes. For example, all CERT literature and application forms contain a positive statement on equal opportunity. Letters stressing equality of opportunity are included in career packages forwarded to second-level schools, FÁS offices, community information centres and public libraries.

CERT strives to maintain a balance in the male/female ratios of trainees on its courses. On Unemployed Programmes the average male/female ratio is 42% male and 58% female; on Initial Training, 38% male and 62% female and on Continuing Training 55% male and 45% female. The only exception is the Bar course which is predominantly male (c.80%) and the Accommodation course which attracts a very high percentage of females (c.99%).

The output levels on CERT's training programmes very closely reflect the employment opportunities within tourism, as evidenced in the 1992 CERT Manpower Survey which showed the male/female ratio in employment to be 42% male and 58% female.

Within the industry itself, CERT aims to encourage equal participation at all grades and to increase employee awareness of training opportunities to ensure that women are not concentrated in the lower paid occupations.

Adult education programmes developed by CERT whose content and structure is particularly suited to women continue to operate in some regional technical colleges. These courses are also run by the Adult Education Section of the Vocational Education Committees.

Under the current NOW Programme CERT, in partnership with FÁS and Teagasc, are involved in developing gender equality systems to ensure good practice in procedures and practices in relation to vocational training. Elements of this project will include management development, training of trainers and the development of monitoring and review systems in relation to gender equality.

Other Positive Action Initiatives

Under the Employment Equality Act, 1977 one of the functions of the Employment Equality Agency is to promote equality of opportunity between men and women in employment. The EEA discharges this function through the development of positive approaches to equality at organisation level in the public and private sector. In particular, the EEA provides advice and assistance to various public and private sector companies in drawing up equal opportunity policies and statements and on methods of developing actions designed to improve the balance of male and female participation in the workforce. The EEA provides assistance in response to individual queries and attends meetings and information sessions with various groups, including trade unions, recruitment agencies, individual firms and students.

The EEA also organises seminars and issues publications in order to raise public awareness of factors affecting the relative position of men and women at work.

As part of the current NOW Programme the EEA have undertaken a joint project with the Institute of Personnel Development to develop special training modules on equality practices to be included in the current certified programme for personnel officers. In addition, specific programmes will be developed for the private and public sector companies to enable organisations to develop staff practices that promote equality of opportunity.

The Commentaries under Articles 2, 5 and 7 refer to positive action measures in the civil service and public sector.

A scheme of grants for lone parents to assist them to return to work or take up second chance educational opportunities is also in operation – see under Article 3.

The Department of Social Welfare operates a Back to Work Allowance Scheme. A person must be 23 years of age or over, be 12 months on the Live Register and be receiving or have an entitlement to Unemployment Assistance between certain amounts or be receiving a Lone Parents Allowance. The scheme allows a person to retain a proportion of their entitlement for 3 years along with secondary benefits while engaged in employment or self-employment. The industries/sectors which can offer suitable employment are those in any of the following areas: Crafts, Community Development Groups, Heritage, Tourism, Voluntary Organisations, Local Enterprises, Horticulture and Fisheries.

(d) ***the right to equal remuneration, including benefits, and to equal treatment in respect of work of equal value, as well as equality of treatment in the evaluation of the quality of work.***

The Anti-Discrimination (Pay) Act, 1974, which came into operation on 31 December, 1974, established the legal right to equal remuneration where a person of one sex employed by the same employer or an associated employer, in the same place of employment, is doing "like work" with a person of the opposite sex. "Remuneration" in this context is defined as including any consideration, whether in cash or in kind, which an employee receives directly or indirectly in respect of her/his employment from her/his employer. The Act sets out certain criteria relating to the definition of "like work", one of which is "where the work performed by one is equal in value to that performed by the other in terms of the demands it makes in relation to such matters as skill, physical or mental effort, responsibility and working conditions".

(e) ***the right to social security, particularly in cases of retirement, unemployment, sickness, invalidity and old age and other incapacity to work, as well as the right to paid leave on the basis of equality of men and women.***

The Irish social welfare code provides the same level of support to men and women in the case of retirement, unemployment, sickness, invalidity, old age and other incapacity to work.

The Holidays (Employees) Act, 1973 provides for paid leave – equivalent to three working weeks where there are twelve qualifying months of service – and public holidays for all workers, irrespective of sex. Conditions governing entitlement apply equally to both sexes.

With effect from 15 April, 1996, where it appears the spouse of a social welfare claimant, rather than the claimant, would benefit most from participation on a training course/scheme, the spouse may participate and receive a training allowance equivalent to the payment received by the Unemployment Assistance/Unemployment Benefit claimant. The claimant will not be entitled to any payment of UA/UB while the spouse is participating on the scheme but may continue to sign for credited contributions. This decision will considerably increase the pool for females eligible to participate on such programmes.

1(f) ***the right to protection of health and to safety in working conditions, including the safeguarding of the function of reproduction.***

States Parties shall take all appropriate measures:

2(d) ***to provide special protection to women during pregnancy in types of work proved to be harmful to them.***

Section 16 of the Employment Equality Act, 1977, includes a saver for special treatment in employment in connection with pregnancy. This section provides that "nothing in this Act shall make it unlawful for an employer to arrange for or provide special treatment to women in connection with pregnancy or childbirth".

The Maternity Protection Act, 1994 provides that a pregnant employee or an employee who has recently given birth or who is breastfeeding shall be granted leave to protect her health and safety, whether because of risk to her in the workplace or arising from night work and where it is not feasible to provide suitable alternative work. For the first three weeks of health and safety leave employees are entitled to receive remuneration from their employers. For the remainder of such leave a social security benefit is payable to eligible employees.

Irish safety and health legislation applies to all workers. In addition, there are extra safety and health provisions relating to women. For example, when granting shift work licences in respect of industrial work, the Department of Enterprise and Employment attaches a recommendation that pregnant workers rostered to work on late shift should have the option to transfer to an alternative shift, depending on medical advice. This recommendation is subject to negotiation between employer and employee. Also, pregnant women are not required to operate VDUs in the Civil Service.

2(a) to prohibit, subject to the imposition of sanctions, dismissal on the grounds of pregnancy or maternity leave and discrimination in dismissals on the basis of marital status.

The Unfair Dismissals Acts, 1977-1995 provide that it shall be unfair to dismiss a worker because of her pregnancy or matters connected therewith or because of the exercise by an employee of her rights under the Maternity Protection Act, 1994. The Employment Equality Act, 1977 prohibits both direct and indirect discrimination on the basis of sex or marital status. On the basis of European Court of Justice case law, the dismissal of an employee on the grounds of pregnancy would be direct discrimination within the meaning of the Act.

In the case of both of these Acts, appropriate sanctions in the form of re-instatement, re-engagement or compensation can be applied for breaches of their provisions.

2(b) to introduce maternity leave with pay or with comparable social benefits without loss of former employment, seniority or social allowances.

The Maternity Protection Act, 1994 incorporates the employment rights aspects of the EU Pregnant Workers Directive into Irish law. The Act covers any employee who is pregnant, who has recently given birth or who is breastfeeding. Pregnant employees are entitled to 14 consecutive weeks' maternity leave, which attracts a social security payment in the majority of cases, and during which all employment rights, other than the right to remuneration, are guaranteed. It also entitles them, at their own option, to additional, unpaid maternity leave of up to four weeks, which must follow on immediately from the maternity leave. During pregnancy and for the 14 week period following the birth, employees are entitled to time off work without loss of pay for ante-natal and post-natal medical visits.

The Act also provides that an employee shall be granted leave to protect her health and safety, whether because of risk to her in the workplace or arising from night work and where it is not feasible to provide suitable alternative work. For the first three weeks of health and safety leave employees are entitled to receive remuneration from their employers. For the remainder of such leave a social security benefit is payable to eligible employees.

Where an employee is absent from work on foot of any absence authorised under the Act, that employee's job is protected and any action seeking to terminate the employment or suspend the employee from the employment is void. Following any such absences an employee has the right to return to work in the same employment and under the same conditions that existed before the leave.

In addition, the Act deems the dismissal of an employee, solely or mainly because of the exercise of any right granted under it, or arising from any matter connected with her pregnancy, having given birth or her breastfeeding to be an unfair dismissal for the purposes of the Unfair Dismissals Act, 1977.

Maternity Benefit is payable to any employee who has been awarded maternity leave under the Maternity Protection Act, 1994. Maternity Benefit is payable for the duration of basic maternity leave entitlement, that is, 14 weeks. If the baby is born later than expected payment of benefit may be extended for up to a further 4 weeks. The claimant must satisfy certain Social Insurance contribution conditions. Weekly payment is made at the rate of 70% of a woman's reckonable weekly earnings in the relevant tax year subject to a minimum and maximum payment.

The Adoptive Leave Act, 1995 came into operation on 20 March, 1995. The Act entitles a woman who is adopting a child (or a man in certain circumstances) to ten weeks adoptive leave and up to four weeks additional adoptive leave in respect of the placement of a child for adoption. The Act ensures that adopting mothers are treated similarly to pregnant workers under the Maternity Protection Act, 1994, as regards maternity leave and protection of employment rights.

Provision was made in the Social Welfare Act, 1995 for the introduction of an Adoptive Benefit scheme for people who are awarded leave under the Adoptive Leave Act, 1995 and who satisfy certain social insurance contribution conditions. The scheme was introduced on 19 April, 1995. Adoptive benefit is payable for a continuous period of 10 weeks from the date of placement of the child, that is, for the duration of the basic 10 weeks adoptive leave entitlement. Rates of payment are similar to Maternity Benefit rates.

2(c) ***to encourage the provision of the necessary supporting social services to enable parents to combine family obligations with work responsibilities and participation in public life, in particular through promoting the establishment and development of a network of child-care facilities.***

It is acknowledged that the provision of childcare services for working parents affects the achievement of real equality in the labour market and that childcare provision in Ireland is among the lowest in the EU. Ireland has the lowest labour market participation rate for mothers with children under 10 in the EU, but the third largest increase in participation, an increase from 18% in 1985 to 30% in 1991. Participation rates for mothers decreases with the number of children.

While the Government encourages the provision generally of childcare facilities through its activities and policies, there is a need for co-operative action by employers, employees and their respective organisations to work with local development and community interests from both the voluntary and public authority sectors to develop childcare provision in response to local needs.

The Government is conscious of the contribution which childcare can make in promoting equal opportunities in employment. While the provision of childcare facilities is primarily a matter for parents, in order to develop a strategy which integrates the different strands of the current arrangements for the development and delivery of childcare and early educational services, an Expert Working Group involving the relevant interests, chaired by the Department of Equality and Law Reform, will be established under the **Partnership 2000** agreement (see Article 1(a)) to devise a national framework for the development of the childcare sector.

In tandem with the development of a childcare strategy, the Government will seek to support the growth of family friendly policies in employment, in line with the recommendations contained in the policy document, **Introducing Family Friendly Initiatives in the Workplace,** issued by the Employment Equality Agency in 1996, and having regard to competitive requirements.

With respect to facilitating staff to combine work and family responsibilities, the job-sharing and career break scheme in the civil service and the wider public sector are of particular relevance. At end December, 1995, there were approximately 2,000 civil servants jobsharing and approximately 900 civil servants on career break. In both cases, the majority of staff availing of the facilities were women. In mid 1995, 64% of local authority staff availing of career breaks were women, and 97% of those job-sharing were women.

The Minister for Health has the main responsibility in relation to day care services for children, with the focus almost exclusively on children at risk. The overall view is that the availability of such facilities will contribute to the alleviation of stress situations and prevent family breakdown which could otherwise lead to the placement of children in care. Health boards make grants towards the running costs of centres providing day care services for children of families in need of special support. The remainder of the funding is provided by parents' subscriptions and fund-raising activities. The establishment of the centres is usually left to voluntary organisations and private individuals.

In addition, local authorities may provide, in connection with their house building programme, such works or services, as will, in the opinion of the authority, serve a beneficial purpose in connection with the requirements of the persons for whom dwellings are being provided. Such services could include crèches.

In 1994 the Department of Education established a pilot programme of pre-school services (Early Start) in line with Government commitment in the White Paper on Education Policy which states that "Early Start is one element of an integrated approach to education, training and employment initiatives for the entire community". The programme initially targeted seven areas of disadvantage. For 1995/6, the programme was further extended. The objective of the Early Start pre-school initiative is to expose young children to an educational programme which will enhance their overall development and lay a foundation for successful educational attainment in future years.

With a small allocation of ERDF (European Regional Development Fund) the NOW programme will develop infrastructure for the support of childcare service provision and enterprise development for women. Models of community based childcare services will be piloted in areas of high unemployment and disadvantage to facilitate the participation of women in vocational training and employment.

Childcare needs are also examined in the context of the EU LEADER programme. This initiative addresses rural development issues, including the contribution of women in that area.

The Minister for Equality and Law Reform introduced a Pilot Childcare Initiative Scheme in 1994 which was continued into 1995, 1996 and 1997. The scheme is intended to assist the initiation of projects for the establishment, on a pilot basis, of childcare measures, in designated disadvantaged areas, to enable local residents to undertake education, training, re-training and employment opportunities which they would be unable to do in the absence of a childcare facility.

The majority of playgroups are initiated and run by parents themselves. The Irish Pre-School Playgroups Association (IPPA), which receives a State grant towards its running expenses, operates a system of voluntary registration. A similar network of Irish language playgroups exists, which also receives financial support from the State. As in other countries, a range of other private arrangements/facilities exist, such as child-minding, private crèches and pre-school facilities. As no system of registration yet exists, however, there is no estimate available of their number. The Child Care Act, 1991 empowers the Minister for Health to make regulations governing the provision of pre-school services. This provision was implemented at the end of 1996. Regulations in pre-school centres for the purpose of securing the health, safety and welfare and promoting the development of children attending pre-school came into effect on 31 December, 1996.

3. ***Protective legislation relating to matters covered in this Article shall be reviewed periodically in the light of scientific and technological knowledge and shall be revised, repealed or extended as necessary.***

Section 35 of the Employment Equality Act, 1977 empowers the EEA, inter alia, to keep under review the working of the 1974 equal pay legislation as well as the 1977 Act itself and to make proposals to the Minister for Equality and Law Reform for amending either or both of those Acts. Proposals to amend these Acts are before Parliament.

Section 38 of the 1977 Act also empowers the EEA to carry out a review of any provision of existing protective legislation where it considers that such a provision is likely to affect or impede the elimination of discrimination in employment or the promotion of equality of opportunity between men and women in employment.

The ongoing review of Ireland's protective legislation has resulted in change and is evidence of the Government's willingness to revise and update protective legislation in the light of scientific and technological knowledge and other relevant factors.

ARTICLE 12

(1) State Parties shall take all appropriate measures to eliminate discrimination against women in the field of health care in order to ensure, on a basis of equality of men and women, access to health care services, including those related to family planning.

(2) Notwithstanding the provisions of paragraph 1 of this Article, State Parties shall ensure women appropriate services in connection with pregnancy, confinement and the post-natal period, granting free services where necessary, as well as adequate nutrition during pregnancy and lactation.

---

(1) State Parties shall take all appropriate measures to eliminate discrimination against women in the field of health care in order to ensure, on a basis of equality of men and women, access to health care services, including those related to family planning.

The health services in Ireland account for a significant share of Government expenditure. Exchequer non-capital spending on health services was almost £2.3bn in 1995, or 15% of all non-capital Exchequer spending. A further £96m was provided for capital expenditure.

Responsibility for health policy at national level lies with the Minister for Health and the Department of Health. The Department of Health assesses the differential effects of policy decisions on women and men when policy changes are proposed. The administration of the health services at regional and local level is the responsibility of eight health boards.

Services in connection with pregnancy, confinement and the post-natal period are available without charge to all Irish women. Ireland has one of the lowest rates of maternal and infant mortality in the world.

There is no discrimination between men and women in the provision of health services, although there are some areas which are of particular concern to women and which will be dealt with here.

A Plan for Women's Health

The Department of Health is finalising a **Plan for Women's Health** and it will be published early in 1997. The plan has been developed in response to a growing concern that women's health needs were not always being met by the health services. In 1993 the Second Commission on the Status of Women recommended that the Department of Health should respond to this concern by publishing a policy document on women's health and engage in extensive consultation with women prior to preparing a plan for women's health.

The first part of the recommendation was implemented with the publication of the Discussion Document – **Developing a Policy for Women's Health** – in June, 1995. The

Discussion Document looked at the health services from a woman's point of view. It analysed the health status of Irish women, pinpointed the main causes of mortality and morbidity among women and identified the scope for preventing premature mortality and increasing health and social gain. The Document provided a detailed analysis of most of the health issues of concern to women and suggested priorities to be addressed in a Plan for Women's Health.

After the publication of the Discussion Document, a process of consultation began with a national conference on women's health on 30 June, 1995. The process was greatly strengthened by the partnership of the National Women's Council. The Council, with funding from the Department of Health, appointed a co-ordinator to work with the statutory side in structuring the consultation. In each health board region the Council appointed "counterparts" to work closely with health boards in organising the consultative process. Each health board in turn appointed a women's health co-ordinator to carry the consultation forward.

Consultation with women on health issues took many forms. Conferences, workshops, exhibitions and seminars were held on the full range of topics in the Discussion Document or on specific topics. Written submissions were also invited from a large number of organisations with an interest in women's health. There was also considerable media coverage and the first debate in the Dáil on women's health began on 9 November, 1995.

The Plan for Women's Health will respond to the issues raised during the consultative process and build on the analysis in the discussion document.

Patient Rights

In accordance with the provisions of the **Charter of Rights for Hospital Patients**, patients have the right to total confidentiality in respect of their medical records. They also have the right to request the hospital to make details of their relevant medical records available to them. Every effort is made to meet patients' wishes in this regard, except where it is considered that this would cause serious harm to their physical or mental health. In such circumstances the information may be communicated through a health professional, normally their family doctor.

The question of introducing further charters to cover groups such as children, expectant mothers, the elderly, the mentally ill and people with a mental or physical disability is being examined in the Department of Health, in the context of its health strategy document.

Preventive Medicine

The Health Promotion Unit of the Department of Health has the task of developing a comprehensive health promotion strategy encompassing schools, the wider community and the workplace. Initiatives are multi-faceted and multi-sectional, involving a wide range of both voluntary and statutory agencies. The Unit was a sponsor of a major national survey on women's health needs carried out by the National Maternity Hospital in 1994, which was published in June, 1996.

Issues of particular relevance to women

Breast Cancer

Ireland ranks mid-way among EU countries in relation to deaths per capita from breast cancer. It is the leading cause of cancer deaths in women in Ireland. In 1994, 657 women died from breast cancer in Ireland; over 50% of these deaths occurred in women aged 65 and over. It is not possible to say what the incidence of breast cancer is in Ireland each year, but this information will be available from 1996 from a new National Cancer Register. As the causes of breast cancer remain to be clearly established, emphasis is placed on early detection at the pre-invasive stage and consequent early treatment.

Mammography in Ireland is used largely as a diagnostic tool for symptomatic or worried women and, in some cases, for "at risk" women. This diagnostic service is available to women on a doctor referral basis. There are currently 18 diagnostic mammography units in the country and expertise has been growing in all aspects of the early detection of breast cancer and its treatment. The Department of Health has supported and continues to support many initiatives in these areas.

The Department of Health supported a major mammographic breast screening programme, the Eccles Breast Screening Programme, as part of a network of pilot schemes on breast cancer screening under way within the European Union. The study was carried out in a defined catchment area, i.e. North Dublin and Cavan/Monaghan, representing both urban and rural populations. All women in the catchment areas aged 50-64 were eligible to attend. Younger women have not been shown to benefit from mammography screening programmes.

The objectives of the Eccles Breast Screening Programme were:

- to evaluate the impact of mammographic screening on mortality from breast cancer among Irish women;
- to document compliance with a breast screening programme in Irish women;
- to compare the specificity, sensitivity and predictive value of the mammography screening programme with that reported internationally.

The Eccles Breast Screening Programme was the first study of this kind undertaken in this country and the results were independently evaluated. The evaluation report supported the decision to introduce a breast screening service, subject to the establishment of a population register. In October 1995, the Minister for Health formally announced the phased expansion of the Programme. The decision to proceed on a phased basis is guided by the need for:

- the achievement of acceptable compliance levels among the target population;
- ongoing evaluation of the programme from a quality assurance perspective; and
- availability of the necessary clinical expertise to conduct the programme.

The first phase of the expanded programme will screen women aged 50-64 years of age residing in the Eastern, North Eastern and Midland Health Board areas. Approximately

120,000 women in the age cohort 50-64, or about half of the women in this country in that age group will be involved in the first phase, the details of which are being finalised. The absence of a population register, together with data protection concerns about the use of information about individuals for purposes other than for which it was given have posed difficulties in planning the first phase. Assuming these difficulties can be overcome, the Minister for Health intends that the first phase of the screening programme would begin in 1997 and that a national screening programme for breast cancer would be in place by early 1999.

The effectiveness of a national breast screening programme in terms of reducing mortality will take many years to establish, in that follow-up must be continued over long periods to compare realistically outcomes in screened and unscreened groups and those of other international studies.

Cervical Cancer
A cervical smear testing service is available to all women on a non-selective basis through their general practitioners, family planning clinics, maternity hospitals and special clinics organised by health boards.

The report of the Working Group on cervical screening was published in November, 1996. The Group looked at all aspects of the cervical screening service to consider what further improvements could be made in this area. The main thrust of the report's conclusions is that cervical screening is a worthwhile preventive health measure when delivered as an organised screening programme for women aged 25-60 years. The recommended interval is 5 years. The report also makes recommendations in the areas of training of personnel, organisation of a cervical screening programme, quality assurance etc. The implementation of the report's recommendations is currently underway and arrangements are being made to prepare the ground for a national cervical screening programme. The target commencement date is not later than 1999 or earlier if resources permit.

Genetic Counselling
A medical genetics centre was established in 1994 in Our Lady's Hospital for Sick Children, Dublin. The counselling service is backed up by a medical genetic laboratory which was opened in 1995. The laboratory offers both a cytogenetic testing and a molecular diagnostic service. The cytogenetic laboratory focuses on testing for chromosomal abnormalities, such as Downs Syndrome, while the molecular laboratory is involved in gene diagnosis, looking at DNA rather than chromosomes. This includes specific inherited disorders such as cystic fibrosis and muscular dystrophy. The laboratory also provides a full range of common genetic tests.

Family Planning
The policy of the Irish Government in relation to family planning is to give individuals the greatest possible freedom to decide the number and spacing of their children.

A range of family planning services is available throughout the country. These services are provided by general practitioners, pharmacists and non-governmental organisations. Comprehensive information and advice in relation to family planning is also readily available through other professional health personnel in both hospital and community settings.

The provision of family planning services is legislated for by the Health (Family Planning) Acts, 1979 to 1993. Under the Health (Family Planning) (Amendment) Act, 1992 health boards are statutorily required to make a comprehensive family planning service available in their areas.

The objective of Ireland's family planning policy is to ensure the provision of comprehensive family planning services to all persons who need such services, on a basis which is equitable and accessible. Health boards are required to ensure that this objective is achieved by implementing an appropriate framework. This will be done through a mix of some or all of the following: health boards' own clinics, general practitioners, non-governmental organisations, maternity hospitals/units and pharmacies, as well as services focused at disadvantaged and/or at-risk groups and at persons with special needs. Additional funds were made available to the health boards in 1995 and in 1996 for the development of comprehensive family planning services. The Department of Health reviews the implementation of the Guidelines on Family Planning on a regular basis to ensure that services are being provided as recommended.

The decline in the numbers of births in recent years, [from 74,064 (1980) to 48,530 (1995) a decrease of 34.5%] and in particular the fall in the size of completed families, indicates the extent to which couples (particularly women) are controlling their fertility. It also illustrates the extent to which education, information and family planning services have impacted on the lives of Irish people.

In 1995, guidelines were issued to the health boards on the development of comprehensive family planning services in their areas. In addition, the range of services available to persons in lower socio-economic groups from their general practitioners was extended.

Abortion

Abortion is prohibited in Ireland by the Offences Against the Person Act, 1861. The prohibition on abortion was enshrined in Article 40.3.3 of the Irish Constitution in 1983, which provides that:

> *The State acknowledges the right to life of the unborn and with due regard to the equal right to life of the mother guarantees in its laws to respect and, as far as practicable, by its laws to defend and vindicate that right.*

The effect of a decision of the Supreme Court in 1992, having regard to Article 40.3.3 of the Constitution, is that termination of pregnancy is permissible in the State where there is a real and substantial risk to the life, as distinct from the health, of the mother which can only be avoided by such termination and that a risk of suicide may constitute a real and substantial risk. The Court decided in the same case that, while an injunction would not be given to restrain a woman from travelling abroad to obtain an abortion where there is a real and substantial risk to her life, such an injunction could be given to restrain travel abroad to obtain an abortion where there was no such risk. In earlier cases the Court also decided that the dissemination of information on abortion was unlawful having regard to Article 40.3.3 of the Constitution.

In 1992, the Constitution was amended by referendum to ensure that Article 40.3.3 could not in future be invoked:

(a) to prevent a woman travelling abroad, whatever the purpose of her journey, or

(b) to prevent the dissemination, in accordance with conditions to be laid down by law, of information about abortion services lawfully available in another state. (The relevant conditions were laid down in legislation enacted in 1995.)

Arising from the Supreme Court decision referred to above, it will be necessary to introduce legislation to regulate the position on abortion, recognising the sensitivity of the issue throughout the community.

While abortion is not available in Ireland, Irish women avail of abortion services in other countries. The best information available is that the Irish abortion rate is 9% of live births, which is a relatively low rate by EU standards. The Government has instituted research in relation to why women choose the option of abortion. More information on the abortion rate will be available from this study.

Dental Health

In 1987 the Government extended free dental treatment to the spouses – mainly wives – of insured workers, which extended eligibility for dental services to approximately 300,000 spouses. During the first two years of its extension the average cost of dental treatment for women under the scheme was 60% greater than for their male counterparts. That differential is now closer to 10%. The Health Promotion Unit of the Department of Health is involved in projects promoting good oral health and hygiene. These initiatives have led to improved dental health among women.

As part of the Health Strategy, the Government announced in May, 1994 a Dental Health Action Plan which will result in the further development of the health board dental services for eligible persons. This plan is being implemented on a phased basis. It includes a new scheme (the Dental Treatment Services Scheme) for the provision of adult dental services with the participation of private dental practitioners. As from 1 June, 1996 routine dental treatment is available under this scheme to all adults with medical card entitlement in the age groups 16-34 and 65 and over.

Mental Health

One in ten Irish people will, at some stage of their lives, suffer from a psychiatric disorder and approximately 16% of the total health non-capital budget is spent on psychiatric services. By international standards Irish rates of mood disorder illness, such as depression and manic depression, are high and depression is the most common mental illness among women.

The report of the Study Group on the Development of the Psychiatric Services, **Planning for the Future**, published in 1984, recommended a shift in the delivery of services for the mentally ill from an institution to a community based service. This report has been adopted by successive Governments and forms the blueprint for the development of psychiatric services into the 21st century. A core recommendation of the report is the provision of a psychiatric service which is fully comprehensive, sector based and integrated with general health. Planning for the Future provides a firm foundation for the monitoring and treatment of mental health problems as they affect women.

Drug Abuse

While there is no hard data on the numbers of women who are misusing drugs, the most recent report by the Health Research Board, **Treated Drug Misuse in the Greater Dublin Area** indicated that 21% of clients attending treatment services were female. In addition to those women who are themselves drug users, the problem of drug misuse touches the lives of many women who take on the role of carers for partners and children who misuse drugs and who frequently raise their grandchildren whose parents are unable to do so through serious illness or death arising from drug misuse and/or drug related AIDS.

In response to Government decisions in February, 1996 health boards are expanding existing services to address drug misuse. The main objective of Government policy is to work with communities to prevent and treat drug misuse and to encourage drug misusers to undertake methadone treatment programmes as a step towards a drug free lifestyle. The Eastern Health Board, which is experiencing the most serious drug problems, is giving a priority to encouraging pregnant drug misusers to attend drug treatment centres. A special community based rehabilitation programme for women, the "SAOL" Project has been developed in conjunction with FÁS. The programme offers stable drug abusers a bridge to mainstream and community based education and training programmes and employment.

Following the **First Report of the Ministerial Task Force on Measures to Reduce the Demand for Drugs**, in October, 1996, £14m was made available for an action programme, £11m of which will go towards drug treatment services and £3m to improve housing estates. A major objective is to eliminate the waiting list for methadone treatment in Dublin by 1997.

Health Policy in HIV/AIDS and other Sexually Transmitted Diseases (STDs)

Up to March, 1996 there was a total of 514 recorded AIDS cases and 281 deaths from AIDS (almost 55% of the total recorded). Intravenous drug users account for the largest number (215 or 42%) of cases of AIDS, homosexuals/bisesuals account for 175 or 34%, heterosexuals for 61 or 12% while the balance of 63 (12%) is made up of haemophiliacs, children and others – table 12.1 refers. Table 12.2 gives an age and gender breakdown of AIDS cases and deaths.

A total of 109,922 tests have been undertaken by the Virus Reference Laboratory for HIV antibodies up to the end of March, 1996 and 1,645 cases have tested positive. The HIV statistics show that IV drug users represent 48% of the total, homosexuals 21%, heterosexuals 15%, and the balance (16%) is made up of haemophiliacs, children and others. Table 12.3 refers.

Table 12.1

AIDS cases and deaths up to 31 March, 1996

	CASES	DEATHS
Homosexuals/Bisexuals	175	87
IV drug users	215	127
Homosexual/Bisexual/IVDU	9	6
Haemophiliacs	31	24
Heterosexuals	61	27
Children born to IV drug users	11	7
Other Children	6	-
Undetermined	6	3
TOTAL	**514**	**281**

Table 12.2

Age breakdown of AIDS cases and deaths by gender to 31 March, 1996

AGE GROUP	AIDS CASES		AIDS DEATHS	
	Male	Female	Male	Female
< 1 year	2	2	1	1
1-4 years	4	5	2	0
5-9 years	3	2	1	2
10-12 years	1	0	1	0
13-14 years	2	0	2	0
15-19 years	8	0	8	0
20-24 years	26	6	16	3
25-29 years	115	33	64	21
30-34 years	113	28	61	17
35-39 years	76	7	38	4
40-49 years	59	2	30	1
50-59 years	18	0	8	0
60+ years	2	0	-	-
TOTAL	**429**	**85**	**232**	**49**

Table 12.3

Cumulative total samples tested in the Virus Reference Laboratory for HIV antibodies (1986 to March,1996)

CATEGORY	Total Tests	Positive Individuals	% of Total
Intravenous Drug Users	**9,839**	**783**	**47.6**
Male	(6,876)	(580)	(74)
Female	(2,848)	(189)	(24)
Unknown	(115)	(14)	(2)
Children at risk	1,692	114	6.9
Homosexuals	4,884	350	21.3
Haemophiliacs	1,106	114	6.9
Haemophiliac Contacts	71	1	—
Hospital Staff/Occupational Hazard/Needlestick	3,529	1	—
* Transfusion	389	1	—
* Blood Donors (specimens referred by Blood Transfusion Service Board)	2,738	20	1.2
* Organ Donors	4,820	0	—
* Visa Requests	12,180	2	0.1
* Insurance	31,562	1	—
* Prisoners	578	16	1.0
Hetero/Risk Unspecified	36,534	242	14.7
TOTAL	**109,922**	**1,645**	—

Note: The above figures which are produced by the Virus Reference Laboratory relate to categories of persons as identified either by patients themselves or by their clinicians.

* Categorised by site reason rather than risk.

The Department of Health has an AIDS strategy in line with recommendations from the World Health Organisation which includes the following:

- education/prevention
- monitoring
- treatment and care of patients
- research.

The Health Promotion Unit is a member of the Education/Prevention sub-committee of the National AIDS Strategy Co-ordinating Committee.

The Unit's convenience advertising initiative involves the placement of female-specific AIDS/HIV education messages in the washroom areas in women's health clinics. Other messages, which are also relevant to women, are in place in third-level colleges and selected entertainment venues. Women are also involved in the delivery of HIV/AIDS information in the Unit's most recent HIV/AIDS prevention radio and television campaign.

In 1990, AIDS education resource materials were disseminated to all second-level schools for use within the wider context of the school's sex and relationship education programme. In-service training was offered to two teachers from each school to assist in the delivery of the programme. The Health Promotion Unit in association with the Irish Association of Social Workers developed a booklet for use by parents of children with HIV. Since 1984, the Unit has widely disseminated a leaflet on sexually transmitted diseases which includes information for women on the cause, symptoms and treatment of various STDs. The family planning legislation has been amended to remove restrictions on the purchase and sale of condoms.

A women's health project based in the Dublin area provides health services, advice and information for women involved in prostitution.

Rape and Sexual Assault

A dedicated unit is located in Dublin for the specialist investigation and treatment of persons who have been sexually assaulted or raped. The unit provides facilities for the effective collection and processing of forensic evidence and a structured environment for the examination and treatment of victims of sexual assault and rape. This service is designed primarily to meet local needs but is also available to residents of other areas. Victims of sexual assault and rape also have access to local general practitioner/general hospital services for medical examination and treatment.

Following medical assessment and treatment in the immediate aftermath of sexual assault and rape, victims are referred for on-going counselling and support. Multidisciplinary teams of health professionals in the regional health boards provide psychological support services for victims of rape and sexual abuse either through specialist counselling centres or the general psychiatric service.

There is an increasing recognition of the complementary role of the voluntary sector and the statutory services in the provision of services to survivors of rape and sexual abuse. There are currently fourteen voluntary rape crisis and counselling centres in receipt of state funding situated in various locations throughout the country. Their services focus predominantly on counselling on a face-to-face basis and by telephone. In line with a recommendation of the Second Commission on the Status of Women, from 1995 onwards secure funding has been made available to the centres through the regional health boards. The linking of the funding of these centres to the health boards will assist in the further integration of the services at a regional level.

A Network of Rape Crisis Centres has been established to encourage networking of the centres around the country.

Female Circumcision
This procedure is never carried out in Ireland.

(2) ***Notwithstanding the provisions of paragraph 1 of this Article, State Parties shall ensure women appropriate services in connection with pregnancy, confinement and the post-natal period, granting free services where necessary, as well as adequate nutrition during pregnancy and lactation.***

A maternity and infant care service is provided free of charge to all women regardless of means. This includes the services of the family doctor during pregnancy and family doctor services for mother and baby for up to six weeks after the birth. It also includes in-patient and out-patient services at either a maternity hospital or in a maternity unit of a general hospital.

There have been substantial improvements in maternal and infant mortality rates in recent decades. Infant mortality has declined from 30.5 per 1,000 live births in 1961 to 8.8 in 1985 and to 6.3 in 1995. Maternal mortality has declined from 0.25 per 1,000 in 1971 to about 0.06 per 1,000 in 1985 and 0.02 per 1,000 births in 1994 with zero in 1993 and 1995. It is generally accepted that, to a large extent, improved specialist ante-natal and obstetric management has brought about a reduction in the rate of maternal mortality.

ARTICLE 13

States Parties shall take all appropriate measures to eliminate discrimination against women in other areas of economic and social life in order to ensure, on a basis of equality of men and women, the same rights, in particular:

(a) ***the right to family benefits;***

(b) ***the right to bank loans, mortgages and other forms of financial credit;***

(c) ***the right to participate in recreational activities, sports and all aspects of cultural life.***

Ireland retains the following reservation in relation to Article 13(a):

> Ireland reserves the right for the time being to maintain provisions of Irish legislation in the area of social security which are more favourable to women than men.

A number of changes have been made since our last report which reflect the changing family structure in Ireland.

In 1989, a social assistance payment was introduced for widowers and deserted husbands with child dependant(s) equal to that available to widows and deserted wives.

In 1990, a new Lone Parent's Allowance was introduced. This scheme incorporated the then existing Unmarried Mother's Allowance, Widower's (non-contributory) Pension and Deserted Husbands Allowance schemes and also the Widow's (non-contributory) Pension, Deserted Wife's Allowance and Prisoners Wife's Allowance schemes in so far as they apply to women with child dependants. Men and women with child dependants are now entitled to claim Lone Parent's Allowance if they are widowed, separated, an unmarried parent or the spouse of a prisoner. The same conditions of entitlement and rates of payment apply to both male and female applicants.

Provision was made in the Social Welfare Act, 1994 for the introduction of a Survivors Pension from October, 1994. Under the new scheme men and women who are widowed qualify for a contributory pension on the same basis. Previously widowers were not entitled to a contributory pension.

The Social Welfare (No. 2) Act, 1995 ensures that divorced people will not be disadvantaged in terms of their social welfare entitlements. Provisions of the Social Welfare Act, 1996, which were brought into force in January, 1997, provide for the introduction of a new One-Parent Family Payment to replace the existing Deserted Wife's Benefit and Lone Parent's Allowance schemes. The main objectives of this new payment, which will be available to both male and female applicants on the exact same basis, are:

- to abolish the concept of desertion within the Irish social security system thereby dispensing with the need for the intrusive questioning associated with proving desertion;

- to provide for equal treatment for male and female one-parent families;
- to be non-judgemental in terms of the reasons for lone parenthood; and
- to improve the incentive for lone parents to take up work opportunities.

Arising from the introduction of the One-Parent Family Payment, the Deserted Wife's Allowance and Prisoner's Wife's Allowance schemes are being discontinued for new applicants. In order to meet the special needs of older women, the Pre-Retirement Allowance scheme has been extended to separated women (and men) aged 55 or over who have not had an attachment to the workforce for a period prescribed by regulations. This will be done in the near future.

Arising from the provisions of the Social Welfare Act, 1996 described above, the primary reason for maintaining the reservation to Article 11.1 is the fact that in the area of family benefits entitlement to Child Benefit is normally vested in the mother. In addition, under transitional arrangements relating to the One Parent Family Payment Scheme some women will continue to receive more favourable treatment until they exhaust their entitlements.

Since July 1994 each full year of homemaking (i.e. time spent in the home while rearing children or while providing full-time care and attention to an incapacitated person) will entitle the person to have a year disregarded for the purposes of determining the yearly average for pension. This continues their social protection and enables them to benefit more fully from a resumption of social insurance on returning to work. The relevant regulations allow women returning to work, who might previously not have qualified for a pension because of a lengthy gap in their Pay Related Social Insurance records, the possibility of now doing so. The age limit for all children was increased to 12 years with effect from 6 April 1995.

The provision of access to pension cover in their own right for women working full-time in the home is being examined.

Family Benefits

Child Benefit is paid universally in respect of all children under the age of 16 or children under the age of 19 who are undergoing full-time education or who are physically or mentally challenged. Entitlement to payment is normally vested in the mother.

There have been significant increases in the rates of Child Benefit in recent years. Taking the last two years together, a 45% increase has been provided in respect of the first two children and a 36% increase for other children.

In the case of multiple births, Child Benefit is payable at double the normal rate in respect of each child, where three or more children are born together. A special once-off grant is payable where four or more children are born together and a once-off grant is also payable on the birth of triplets.

The Government is committed to substantial reform of the system of income support for children, with the particular objective of making such support more neutral vis-a-vis the parents' employment status. A key part of this are the improvements to Child Benefit as outlined above.

The purpose of Family Income Supplement (FIS) is to create an incentive for workers with families who are in low paid employment and who would otherwise be better off on a social welfare payment to remain at work. It is therefore a statutory condition for receipt of the scheme that a claimant be employed in remunerative employment as an employee for at least 19 hours per week every week. From June, 1996 the employment requirement was reduced to three months, from the previous six month requirement. Job-sharers are also included for the first time since June, 1996. The hours worked by a person's spouse/partner can be combined.

A Supplementary Welfare Allowance Scheme is administered by the health boards under the general direction of the Minister for Social Welfare. Under this scheme, every person in the State, apart from those who are specifically excluded by the legislation i.e. persons in full-time employment, full-time education, people involved in a trade dispute (but the latter may be entitled to assistance in respect of the needs of their dependants), whose means are insufficient to meet her/his needs and those of her/his dependants is entitled to supplementary welfare allowance.

There is also a comprehensive range of social welfare schemes designed to provide income and other supports either on a contributory or non-contributory basis. Benefits in kind such as free electricity and telephone rental allowance, free TV licence and fuel allowance are available to certain Social Welfare pensioners over 66 and certain categories under 66. Free travel is available to all persons over age 66 and certain categories under that age.

Carer's Allowance is paid to persons (80% of whom are women) who are providing certain people with full-time care and attention and whose income falls below a certain limit. Considerable improvements have been made in recent years to this scheme in respect of the means test and earnings disregards. In addition, rates of payment were increased in 1996 by 8% which is well in excess of the general 3% increase in other Social Welfare payments.

Tables 13.1 to 13.4 provide details of social welfare payments.

Financial Credit

There is no specific legislation on the Irish Statute book which expressly regulates the obligations of private individuals to accord equality in the areas covered by Article 13(b) and (c). It is for this reason that, on acceding to this Convention, Ireland lodged the following reservation in the matter:

> *The question of supplementing the guarantee of equality contained in the Irish Constitution with special legislation governing access to financial credit and other services and recreational activities, where these are provided by private persons, organisations or enterprises is under consideration. For the time being Ireland reserves the right to regard its existing law and measures in this area as appropriate for the attainment in Ireland of the objectives of the Convention.*

With regard to complaints concerning access by women to financial credit, the level of such complaints has not been extensive. In addition, in October, 1990 an Ombudsman for Credit Institutions was appointed thereby providing a ready means of redress against any discriminatory practice.

Notwithstanding the above, the Government is committed to bringing forward equal status legislation which will prohibit discrimination on the basis of, inter alia, sex, marital status and family status, in relation to goods, facilities, services and education, including access to financial credit and sports facilities. When this legislation is enacted the Government will be enabled to withdraw its reservation to Article 13(b) and (c).

Sports

The Department of Education operates a positive action programme in allocating funding to women's sports organisations and grants are not available to sports organisations which operate discriminatory policies.

Cultural Life

Funding for the contemporary arts in Ireland is administered by the Arts Council, a body established to stimulate public interest in the arts, promote the knowledge, appreciation and practice of the arts, and assist in improving the standards of the arts.

The Arts Council is committed to the ideal of a society based on principles of equality and equal opportunity. The Council is committed to a policy of equality of opportunity in its employment practices, and, in particular, aims to ensure that no potential or actual employee receives more or less favourable treatment on the grounds of race, colour, ethnic or national origins, marital status, gender, sexual orientation, age, disability or religious affiliation. It is a condition of receipt of grant-aid that organisations assisted by the Council agree to avoid any form of discriminatory practice and to pay particular regard to promoting equal opportunities in all areas of their work.

The principle of Access, which is a key strategic objective of the Arts Council's **The Arts Plan 1995-1997** together with the **Cultural Development Incentive Scheme** up to the year 1999 (see commentary on Article 3), will contribute greatly to the modification of cultural patterns of conduct of women and men. The flourishing of arts and cultural activity which these measures will facilitate will, it is considered, fully respond to the objectives of this Article.

Table 13.1(a)

Deserted Wife's Allowance – Number of Beneficiaries at 31 December								
Beneficiaries	**1989**	**1990***	**1991**	**1992**	**1993**	**1994**	**1995**	**1996**
Deserted wives	5,271	1,793	1,895	1,971	2,051	2,095	2,125	2,138
Dependent children of wives	8,816	—	—	—	—	—	—	—
Total	**14,087**	**1,793**	**1,895**	**1,971**	**2,051**	**2,095**	**2,125**	**2,138**
Social Assistance (unmarried parents) Allowance								
Unmarried parents	16,564	18,761	21,366	24,077	26,735	29,987	33,824	37,506
Dependent children	21,291	24,400	28,181	32,009	35,888	40,506	46,124	51,664
Total	**37,855**	**43,161**	**49,547**	**56,086**	**62,623**	**70,493**	**79,948**	**89,170**
Prisoner's Wife's Allowance								
Prisoners wives	225	9	12	9	8	7	8	6
Dependent children of wives	683	—	—	—	—	—	—	—
Total	**908**	**9**	**12**	**9**	**8**	**7**	**8**	**6**

* From 1990, recipients of Deserted Wife's Allowance and Prisoner's Wife's Allowance with children transferred to Lone Parent's Allowance. Figures for unmarried mothers from 1990 include men and women on the Unmarried Parent's portion of the Lone Parent's Allowance.

Table 13.1(b)

Lone Parents Allowance 1991-1996, Recipient Numbers						
Type of Benefit	**1991**	**1992**	**1993**	**1994**	**1995**	**1996**
LPA (Unmarried parent)	21,366	24,077	26,735	29,987	33,824	37,506
Dependent children	28,181	32,009	35,888	40,506	46,124	51,664
LPA (Separated spouse)	5,391	6,438	7,585	8,714	10,117	11,268
Dependent children	13,090	15,472	18,071	20,44	23,428	25,887
LPA (Widowed)	2,263	2,277	2,219	1,880	1,744	1,685
Dependent children	4,782	4,886	4,667	3,859	3,486	3,384
LPA (Prisoners spouse)	164	135	114	119	94	98
Dependent children	498	365	332	332	285	252
Total Female Recipients	**28,033**	**31,643**	**35,221**	**39,384**	**44,466**	**49,127**
Total Male Recipients	**1,151**	**1,284**	**1,432**	**1,316**	**1,313**	**1,430**
Total Recipients	**29,184**	**32,927**	**36,653**	**40,700**	**45,779**	**50,557**
Total Children	**46,551**	**52,732**	**58,958**	**65,141**	**73,323**	**81,187**

Table 13.2

Disability and Maternity								
	1989	1990	1991	1992	1993	1994	1995	1996
Persons in receipt of disability benefit at beginning of January	55,521	52,765	49,726	47,733	43,924	41,869	41,830	42,460
Male	29,152	26,015	25,258	23,395	20,846	19,165	18,611	18,782
Female	26,369	25,850	24,468	24,338	23,078	22,704	23,219	23,678
Particulars of Families, Children and Cost of Children's Allowances								
Families	471,837	473,232	476,411	476,086	482,300	482,592	491,520	497,252
Children	1,122,702	1,108,561	1,097,447	1,078,690	1,074,735	1,005,156	1,065,471	1,060,496
Cost of Allowances (m)	£207.7	£209.7	£215.8	£219.1	£231.3	£265.5	£301.0	N/A
Deserted Wives' Benefit								
(a) Deserted Wives	9,400	10,462	11,358	12,270	12,949	13,662	14,284	14,738
(b) Dependent children of wives	17,718	19,239	20,266	21,611	21,994	22,282	22,291	21,874
Total (a) + (b)	**27,188**	**29,701**	**31,624**	**33,881**	**34,943**	**35,944**	**36,575**	**36,612**

Table 13.3

Widows' and orphans' pensions: number of beneficiaries at 31 December 1989-1996								
	1989	1990*	1991	1992	1993	1994	1995	1996
Contributory Pensions								
Widows	83,162	84,011	84,493	85,503	86,371	90,671**	94,713**	96,107**
Dependent children of widows	14,725	14,131	13,383	13,475	13,207	15,259	16,529	16,849
Orphans	718	723	697	698	675	709	765	808
Non-Contributory Pensions								
Widows	19,002	17,877	18,287	18,677	18,825	19,043	19,108	19,046
Dependent children of widows	3,349	–	–	–	–	–	–	–
Orphans	150	144	143	172	223	237	299	340
Total								
Widows	102,164	101,888	102,780	104,180	105,196	109,714	113,821	115,153
Dependent children of widows	18,074	14,131	13,383	13,475	13,207	15,259	16,529	16,849
Orphans	868	867	840	870	898	946	1,064	1,148
Total	**121,106**	**116,886**	**117,003**	**118,525**	**119,301**	**125,919**	**131,414**	**133,150**

* From 1990, recipients of non-contributory widows pension with children transferred to the Lone Parent's Allowance.

** Includes widowers from 28 October, 1994.

Table 13.4

Supplementary Welfare Allowance Scheme and Expenditure in each year as shown								
	1989	**1990**	**1991**	**1992***	**1993****	**1994****	**1995****	**1996**
Services and Expenditure								
Persons in receipt of Supplementary Welfare Allowance on 31 March	11,205	12,572	14,208	13,688	16,500	16,800	16,552	N/A
National Fuel Scheme	210,402	219,744	230,000	245,507	255,000	263,600	274,500	N/A
Supplementary Welfare Allowance								
Expenditure (£000) for each year ending in December	36,485	48,900	61,925	89,598	97,759	108,106	119,539	N/A
National Fuel Scheme (£000)	25,901	29,506	34,422	37,356	37,525	39,903	42,746	N/A
Social Assistance (Single Woman's Allowance) number of beneficiaries at 31 December								
	2,366	2,187	1,981	1,809	—	—	—	—

* Recipients of Single Woman's Allowance transferred to Pre-Retirement Allowance from 5 November, 1992.

** Figures for Single Woman's Allowance are end December figures.

ARTICLE 14

1. *States Parties shall take into account the particular problems faced by rural women and the significant roles which rural women play in the economic survival of their families, including their work in the non-monetized sectors of the economy, and shall take all appropriate measures to ensure the application of the provisions of this Convention to women in rural areas.*

2. *States Parties shall take all appropriate measures to eliminate discrimination against women in rural areas in order to ensure, on a basis of equality of men and women, that they participate in and benefit from rural development and, in particular, shall ensure to such women the right:*

   (a) *to participate in the elaboration and implementation of development planning at all levels;*

   (b) *to have access to adequate health care facilities, including information, counselling and services in family planning;*

   (c) *to benefit directly from social security programmes;*

   (d) *to obtain all types of training and education, formal and non-formal, including that relating to functional literacy, as well as, inter alia, the benefit of all community and extension services, in order to increase their technical proficiency;*

   (e) *to organise self-help groups and co-operatives in order to obtain equal access to economic opportunities through employment or self-employment;*

   (f) *to participate in all community activities;*

   (g) *to have access to agricultural credit and loans, marketing facilities, appropriate technology and equal treatment in land and agrarian reform as well as in land resettlement schemes;*

   (h) *to enjoy adequate living conditions, particularly in relation to housing, sanitation, electricity and water supply, transport and communications.*

---

1. *States Parties shall take into account the particular problems faced by rural women and the significant roles which rural women play in the economic survival of their families, including their work in the non-monetized sectors of the economy, and shall take all appropriate measures to ensure the application of the provisions of this Convention to women in rural areas.*

In Ireland, according to the 1991 Census of Population the aggregate town populations was 57%, with 43% living outside urban areas. In 1901, 28.3% of the total population was in aggregate town areas.

According to the 1991 Census there were 1,314,565 women aged fifteen years or over living in Ireland and, of these more than half a million (526,853) were living in rural areas, i.e. 40% of all women aged 15 years and over. Men outnumber women in all groups up to age 65 in rural areas; after age 65 women outnumber men. The main demographic indicators for rural and urban areas are shown in Tables 14.1 and 14.2.

Table 14.1

Demographic indicators for rural and urban female population aged 15 years and over, 1991

	Rural	Urban	Ireland
Females per 1,000 males	939	1,068	1,011
% Single	30.0	38.8	35.3
% Married	55.4	47.6	50.7
% Separated	1.4	3.4	2.6
% Widowed	13.3	10.1	11.4
% 65 years +	20.0	15.7	17.4

Source: Census of Population, Vol. 2, 1991

Table 14.2

Population of aggregate town area and aggregate rural area by sex and marital status, 1991

	Urban				Rural			
	Male		Female		Male		Female	
	Under 65	Over 65	Under 65	Over 65	Under 65	Over 65	Under 65	Over 65
Single	550,995	13,593	528,618	28,260	438,455	28,709	347,623	17,192
Ever Married (excl widowed)	338,216	49,088	365,288	36,567	243,004	53,419	264,043	34,946
Widowed	5,382	14,837	21,061	58,795	3,641	14,079	16,493	53,415
Total	**894,593**	**77,518**	**914,967**	**123,622**	**685,100**	**96,207**	**628,159**	**105,553**

Source: Central Statistics Office, Census of Population, 1991, 1st Series

The number of women in the Labour Force who classified themselves as having an agricultural occupation in 1993 was 11,000 or 2.7% of the female labour force, compared to 3.4% in 1987 and 14.7% in 1973.

A Census of Agriculture was conducted in June, 1991 by the Central Statistics Office which provided for the first time comprehensive information of the work input of women on Irish farms. All persons aged 15 years and over who contributed to farm work during the previous 12 months were separately identified and details of their labour input obtained.

The total farm labour force in 1991 was as follows:

Table 14.3

Total Farm Labour Force

	Number of Persons	Total AWU*	Average AWU per person	% with Other Gainful Activity
Farm holders	169,893	142,948	0.84	26.6
Holders' spouses	72,080	52,989	0.74	26.5
Other family members	57,314	38,238	0.67	41.7
Total family members	299,287	234,176	0.78	31.9
Regular non-family workers	13,442	11,023	0.82	-
TOTAL	**312,729**	**245,199**	**0.78**	

Table 14.4

Persons working on farm holdings, 1991

	Women	AWU	Men	AWU
Holders	16,414	11,675	153,479	131,273
Spouses	64,230	46,752	7,850	6,237
Other family workers	10,787	5,937	46,527	32,301
Non-family	1,886	1,248	11,556	9,775
TOTAL	**93,317**	**65,612**	**219,412**	**179,587**

* Annual Work Unit – 1 annual work unit = 1,800 hours or more of labour input per person per annum.

Source: Census of Agriculture, 1991, Central Statistics Office

There are wide differences within the farming sector in Ireland in terms of the size of the farming operation and farm income. Many farm families rely on off-farm income or social welfare payments to supplement their farm income. There were approximately 9,000 recipients of Smallholders Unemployment Assistance at the end of December, 1996.

It is difficult to estimate the precise number of farm women in Ireland as farm wives are not counted as a separate category in the Population Census or Labour Force Statistics. The Census of Agriculture, 1991 showed that there were 170,578 holdings, of which 16,414 were in women's hands. As unpaid work is not categorised, most farm wives are classified as "engaged on home duties". The 1991 Census of Agriculture found that about 91,431 female family members contribute to work on the family farm, the largest group of whom is spouses (64,230) accounting for about 73% of the total work input of female family members, or about 27.5% of total family work input. The Irish Farmers' Association put a value of £467.5m on this work. Table 14.4 provides a breakdown of persons working on farm holdings, by sex, in 1991.

While the farm is seen as a family operation the husband has traditionally held the position of "head of the farm". In terms of actual labour and the provision of support services the farm wife's contribution to the family farm may be the same, or greater, than that of her husband.

Very few women own farms or have joint ownership rights. According to the 1991 Census of Agriculture, less than 10% of farm-holders were female. Land transfer has tended to operate on a patrilineal basis. The 1991 Census of Agriculture shows that over 75% of land owned by the current owner was acquired through inheritance (45%) or by family transfer. Most married women "marry into" a farm which their husband has acquired as a gift or inheritance and partnerships and co-ownerships are comparatively rare. Unless a couple decide to transfer the farm into joint ownership most women do not have title to the family farm. The Government abolished stamp duty on gifts between spouses in 1990, so there is no cost disincentive to transferring the farm into joint ownership, but joint ownership is still relatively unusual.

2(a) the right to participate in the elaboration and implementation of development planning at all levels.

In the area of land-use planning and development control, there is no distinction between urban and rural areas, nor is there any differentiation between the sexes in the application of the relevant legislation. The Local Government (Planning and Development) Acts, 1963-1993 provide for public participation in the formulation of the policy and objectives of local development plans. The plans are made and implemented by the local authorities; these bodies are democratically elected by adult suffrage and candidature is open to both sexes. The Planning Acts do not contain any discriminatory clauses against women.

2(b) to have access to adequate health care facilities, including information, counselling and services in family planning.

Rural women enjoy the same health care facilities and services as their urban counterparts, as detailed in the commentary under Article 12. The centralisation of hospital services means that rural women may have to travel longer distances for maternity services or other hospital based services. See also commentary under Articles 3 and 12.

Safety and accident prevention on the family farm is a specific health issue affecting farm women. The National Authority for Occupational Safety and Health and Teagasc (the agriculture and food development authority) work closely with farming organisations to produce effective safety programmes.

Farm relief services are well-developed and are available to help farmers – female and male – in circumstances such as sickness and accident.

2(c) ***to benefit directly from social security programmes.***

There is no distinction between women from urban or rural areas for the purposes of entitlement to social security.

EU Directives in the area of social security are based on the principle of equal treatment between spouses. Directive 86/613/EC on the application of the principle of equal treatment between men and women engaged in an activity, including agriculture, in a self employed capacity, and on the protection of self-employed women during pregnancy and motherhood states that Member States should enable spouses to join a contributory social security scheme voluntarily where they are not protected under the self-employed workers' social security scheme.

Self-employed persons, including farmers, are normally insurable for social insurance as self-employed persons. A spouse working in the family business is not normally insurable. However, where a farmer's wife (or a spouse in any other business) is a registered partner in the business and receives half of the income from that business, which is more than £2,500 per annum, she can be classed as being a self employed person and pay the appropriate insurance contributions as a self-employed person. Women, including farmers' wives, may qualify for payments such as Unemployment Assistance or Supplementary Welfare Allowance subject to a means test.

In relation to the EU Directive on the implementation of equal treatment for men and women in statutory and occupational benefit schemes, men and women are both entitled to a Widows or Widowers pension under social security legislation. Similar provision applies to occupational benefit schemes under the Pensions Act, 1990.

2(d) ***the right to obtain all types of training and education, formal and non-formal, including that relating to functional literacy as well as, inter alia, the benefit of all community and extension services, in order to increase their technical proficiency.***

There is no discrimination between urban and rural women in access to education as detailed in the commentary on Article 10.

The Department of Education funds a countrywide adult literacy and community education programme through the VECs. The majority of participants are women. Literacy tuition for adults is also provided as part of programmes in which there is a strong participation of women.

Rural girls tend to spend longer in the formal education system than rural boys up to the end of second level. However, more boys continue to third level, 4.2% compared to 3.8% of rural girls.

Teagasc – the agriculture and food development authority – has responsibility for agricultural training for farming women and men and courses are open to both. Participation in Teagasc courses has been dominated by men and Teagasc is reviewing the curriculum with a view to increasing the participation of women. Training brochures are designed to encourage women to enter courses.

Most of Teagasc's training is provided through the "Young Entrant Training Programme and the Adult Farmer Programme". Table 14.5 shows the participation of women on these programmes.

Table 14.5

Teagasc Training Programmes for Farmers

Young Entrant Training Programme	**% women participating**
- Agriculture	4.4
- Horticulture	25.0
- Specialised Courses	16.0
- Farm Apprenticeship	1.5
Adult Farmer Programme	**14.0**

Source: Women and Rural Development – Report of the Joint Oireachtas Committee on Women's Rights, January, 1994.

Attendance at courses relating to alternative enterprises such as Rural Tourism, Rural Based Food Enterprise, Horses, Deer Production and Forestry, which are promoted by Teagasc, have had participation by women in excess of 50%.

Teagasc operated a NOW Programme specifically geared to providing support and training for women. The programme also involved a study to determine how participation by women in Teagasc could be improved.

FÁS courses are open to rural women on the same basis as urban women but accessibility and lack of support services can act as a disincentive. Statistics for women's participation on an urban/rural basis are not available.

Women represented 39% of undergraduate students entering Agricultural Science and Forestry degree level courses in 1992-93.

2(e) ***the right to organise self-help groups and co-operatives in order to obtain equal access to economic opportunities through employment or self-employment.***

There are no legal barriers preventing rural women from forming associations, co-operatives or self-help groups. However, there are few women in evidence in such organisations. In this farming organisations reflect the same pattern as other social partners.

Changes in the European Union have led to a new emphasis on rural development as a way of strengthening rural economies. In this context, alternative enterprises, tourism and heritage development, community enterprises, and small business development, are being encouraged at EU and national level, particularly in the Operational Programmes associated with Structural Funds.

Rural women are involved in tourism and enterprise projects and in locally based rural development initiatives to a considerable extent. Rural development has also been identified as a specific objective in the NOW Programme and measures funded include leadership and enterprise training for rural women, as well as assistance with co-operative and business establishment.

For over eighty years the Irish Countrywomen's Association has made a notable contribution to the lives of rural women and has progressed and changed over the years as rural life has changed. Assertiveness courses are now promoted alongside the teaching of arts and crafts, and the ICA uses the strength of its large membership to become involved in social and economic policy issues. One outcome is that women are forming groups related to needs in their own communities. These groups are mainly involved in adult education and personal development through programmes based on needs identified by the women themselves.

A considerable number of local ICA groups receive grants under the Womens/Lone Parents Grant schemes.

2(f) ***the right to participate in all community activities.***

There are no legal barriers to the participation of rural women in community activities.

Women – urban and rural – are more likely than men to be involved in social, religious, educational, cultural and community organisations. Women form the mainstay of parent/teacher associations, caring organisations and self-help groups, which help shape society and effect social reforms. However, women are not to the forefront in farming organisations and there is a perception of farming as a male domain.

2(g) ***the right to have access to agricultural credit and loans, marketing facilities, appropriate technology and equal treatment in land and agrarian reform as well as in land resettlement schemes.***

Access by women generally to credit is dealt with under Article 13 (b).

Female farmers in Ireland have access to the same financial facilities as their male counterparts.

The aim of Government land policy is to ensure, as far as practicable, that the ownership and management of agricultural land is in the hands of those best fitted to work it to optimal advantage. In implementing this policy the Government does not discriminate against women.

2(h) ***the right to enjoy adequate living conditions, particularly in relation to housing, sanitation, electricity and water supply, transport and communications.***

The provision of social housing in Ireland (i.e. housing for those unable to secure adequate accommodation from their own resources) is a function of local authorities. Local authorities either provide accommodation directly or increasingly in recent years assist the provision of social housing by voluntary or co-operative housing organisations.

The Department of the Environment has issued comprehensive guidelines setting out the procedures and standards to which local authorities must comply in the planning and construction of all housing schemes provided by them, including adequate and proper facilities, proximity to existing services and provision of a range of house designs and sizes to cater for the need of occupants.

The overall strategy of local authorities in planning housing developments is to secure the best use of available land together with variety of layout, good design and a high standard of construction, and to ensure that the social objectives of the housing programme are met in the fullest possible manner.

Since the mid 1980s increasing emphasis has been placed on the development of infill sites integrated with existing communities and large scale developments in peripheral locations have been avoided as far as possible.

The necessity to take measures to mitigate the effects of undue social segregation in housing is also recognised and local authorities are required by law to develop strategies to tackle the issue.

In addition, as part of the overall drive to improve the environment of public housing estates, all local authorities have been legally obliged to prepare formal statements of their management and maintenance policies. Tenant participation in these functions can be expected to have a beneficial effect.

Significant funding is being provided for the implementation of an accelerated programme of remedial works to local authority dwellings and towards the provision of bathrooms in local authority dwellings still lacking these facilities.

There are currently over 800 public water supply systems serving about 80% of the population (2.82 million). The remaining 20% are served from private group schemes or individual private sources, mainly wells and boreholes. It is estimated that some 98% of all dwellings in the State have piped water supplies of one sort or another.

Approximately 600 public sewerage systems service mainly the urban population and a substantial proportion of industry. Some 2.32m persons (resident population) are connected to sewage collection systems.

Under the National Development Plan 1994-1999 the Irish Government has, inclusive of EU co-financing commitments, committed in excess of £600m to extending and improving water supply and sewerage schemes nationally to the end of the decade.

The Water Services Investment Programme, 1996 is being undertaken for the benefit of all persons served irrespective of gender or social status. The main objectives of the Programme, in line with those of the Community Support Framework for Ireland, and the Operational Programme for Environmental Services 1994-1999, are:

- to improve the quality of public and group water supplies to ensure that the existing 94% level of compliance of public water supplies with the EU Drinking Water Directive is increased to full compliance by the end of the decade;

- to increase the proportion of urban waste water being treated in accordance with the requirements of the EU Urban Waste Water Treatment Directive from some 20% of the load to approximately 80%;

- to meet identified urban and rural needs for services of acceptable quality and quantity;

- to end the dumping of sewage sludge at sea by end 1998;

- as far as possible, to eliminate serious pollution of rivers, currently 1% of monitored river channel length, and to reverse and minimise slight and moderate pollution, currently 21% of monitored river channel length.

In the rural context the following elements of the Water Services Investment Programme should be noted:

Group Water Schemes

The Group Water Scheme Programme, which is largely connected with the supply of water to rural households and farms, is an integral part of national domestic water supply policy. Under the group water scheme programme, groups of householders (2 or more households, some groups with over 1,000 members) come together to provide piped water supplies through co-operative effort.

Grants of up to £1,600 per house and £1,200 per farm subject to a maximum of 75% of cost (whichever is lesser) are available under the programme. To date, over 150,000 rural households have been connected to some 9,000 group water schemes. Expenditure on the Programme in 1995 was £4.7 million.

Small Schemes Programme
This programme is primarily designed to meet the needs of rural areas and Exchequer grants of up to £150,000 (75% of cost of scheme or £75,000 whichever is lesser) are made available to each county council per annum for approved water services schemes.

In 1995, 45 schemes were approved nationally at a total cost of £4.5m with a grant requirement of £3.1m.

Water Services Sub-Programmes
A number of sub-programmes have been initiated by the Department of the Environment in 1996 to facilitate social and economic development in rural areas particularly.

Innovative reedbed and natural wetland sewage treatment systems are being considered to address pollution problems in rural areas, where low density populations make conventional engineering solutions uneconomic. This initiative will complement initiatives under the Operational Programme for Local Urban and Rural Development in improving local services and amenities given that self-purification reedbed sewerage technology is particularly suited to small rural settlements.

Under the Resorts Initiative Sub-Programme proposals for improved water supply and sewerage services in nine well known coastal resort areas were approved. The initiative will cost in excess of £3m over two years and its wide range of measures includes new and upgraded sewage collection systems and treatment plants, storm overflow and outfall provision and water mains replacement and leakage and pressure control infrastructure.

Under the Water Conservation Sub-Programme a number of water conservation projects are ongoing or planned. In addition an integrated national water conservation strategy is planned to include a nationwide water audit. The aim of the strategy is to more efficiently manage existing water resources and defer costly infrastructure provision in order to facilitate improved quality and quantity of water to the benefit of all sectors in the community.

ARTICLE 15

1. *States Parties shall accord to women equality with men before the law.*

2. *States Parties shall accord to women, in civil matters, a legal capacity identical to that of men and the same opportunities to exercise that capacity. In particular, they shall give women equal rights to conclude contracts and to administer property and shall treat them equally in all stages of procedure in courts and tribunals.*

3. *States Parties agree that all contracts and all other private instruments of any kind with a legal effect which is directed at restricting the legal capacity of women shall be deemed null and void.*

4. *States Parties shall accord to men and women the same rights with regard to the law relating to the movement of persons and the freedom to choose their residence and domicile.*

Equality before the law is a fundamental right guaranteed under the Irish Constitution. Article 40.1 states, inter alia, that

> *All citizens shall, as human persons, be held equal before the law.*

At all stages of procedures in courts and tribunals women are treated equally to men. Under the Married Women's Status Act, 1957 a husband and wife are treated as two separate persons for the purposes of acquisition of property. A married woman can acquire, hold and dispose of property and is capable of contracting and being rendered personally liable in respect of her contracts and debts.

Section 36 of the Family Law Act, 1995 replaces section 12 of the Act of 1957 and provides new powers to the courts for the determination of questions between spouses as to the title to or possession of any property that is in dispute.

Under Irish law the parties of either sex to a contract are entitled to regulate their affairs as they wish, subject to the law on duress. The following reservation to paragraph 3 of this Article was entered when Ireland acceded to the Convention:

> With regard to paragraph 3 of this Article, Ireland reserves the right not to supplement the existing provisions in Irish law which accord women a legal capacity identical to that of men with further legislation governing the validity of any contract or other private instrument freely entered into by a woman.

It was considered that the wording of Article 15.3 could create difficulties by limiting the right freely to enter into contracts. A possible interpretation was that women would not be free to waive their rights or surrender part of their legal capacity in a contract or other private instrument. Under existing contract law, both men and women enjoy this freedom. This reservation may be due to an excess of caution and the question of its removal, given recent interpretation of the Article, is under review.

Under Irish law women and men are free to choose their place of domicile and residence. The Irish Courts have established the right to free movement within the State as an instance of "the many personal rights of the citizen which follow from the Christian and democratic nature of the State which are not mentioned in Article 40 [of the Constitution] at all" (Ryan v Attorney-General, 1965 Irish Reports 294). The right to travel outside the State has also been identified under Article 40 of the Constitution.

Article 16

1. *States Parties shall take all appropriate measures to eliminate discrimination against women in all matters relating to marriage and family relations and in particular shall ensure, on a basis of equality of men and women:*

   (a) *the same right to enter into marriage;*

   (b) *the same right freely to chose a spouse and to enter into marriage only with their free and full consent;*

   (c) *the same rights and responsibilities during marriage and at its dissolution ;*

   (d) *the same rights and responsibilities as parents, irrespective of their marital status, in matters relating to their children; in all cases the interests of the children shall be paramount;*

   (e) *the same rights to decide freely and responsibly on the number and spacing of their children and to have access to the information, education and means to enable them to exercise these rights;*

   (f) *the same rights and responsibilities with regard to guardianship, wardship, trusteeship and adoption of children, or similar institutions where these concepts exist in national legislation; in all cases the interests of the children shall be paramount;*

   (g) *the same personal rights as husband and wife, including the right to choose a family name, a profession or occupation;*

   (h) *the same rights for both spouses in respect of the ownership, acquisition, management, administration, enjoyment and disposition of property, whether free of charge or for a valuable consideration.*

2. *The betrothal and the marriage of a child shall have no legal effect, and all necessary action including legislation, shall be taken to specify a minimum age for marriage and to make the registration of marriages in an official registry compulsory.*

Commentary on legislative and other measures taken to protect women from violence in the home, as requested by the Committee on the Elimination of Discrimination Against Women in General Recommendation 12, follows.

Domestic Violence

Statutory Provisions

Legislative provisions to combat domestic violence have been put in place in Ireland over the past number of years by way of legislation on barring orders, protection orders, child care, rape and indecent assault and the giving of evidence by spouses.

The most widely availed of remedy in cases of inter-spousal violence is the civil law remedy of a barring order first introduced by way of legislation in 1976. That legislation was replaced in 1981. A comprehensive review of the law in relation to the protection of persons from domestic violence was carried out in the Department of Equality and Law Reform taking into account representations made by interested groups and recommendations contained in reports of the Law Reform Commission[1] and the National Second Commission on the Status of Women. Following this review the Domestic Violence Bill was initiated in 1995 and was enacted in 1996. The Act repealed and re-enacted with amendments the 1981 Act.

Barring orders may be granted by the courts on the application of a spouse against the other spouse where the safety or welfare of the applicant spouse and any children warrant it. The court can direct the respondent spouse to leave the place where the applicant spouse or child resides.

Between the making of an application for a barring order and its determination the courts are empowered to grant a protection order as an interim measure. A protection order prohibits the respondent spouse from using or threatening to use violence against, molesting or putting in fear the applicant spouse or a child – it does not operate to bar the respondent spouse from the home.

The barring order remedy was limited under the Act of 1981 to situations of interspousal violence, including violence against any children by either spouse – it did not apply to the increasingly common situation where couples, although not married to each other, are living together as husband and wife.

The 1996 Act also provides for the granting of a protection type order (called a safety order) in its own right and not as, heretofore, an interim measure pending the granting of a barring order. The class of persons covered by the legislation has been extended to include cohabitants and other members of the household, subject to conditions. The District Court's power to grant a barring order – limited to twelve months under the 1981 Act, renewable on application for a further twelve months – is now three years and health boards, subject to certain conditions, are empowered to apply for orders to protect victims of domestic violence. New powers of arrest are given to the Gardaí under the new Act. The penalties for contravening a barring order or a protection order are increased – the fine from £200 to £1,500 and the term of imprisonment from six months to twelve months.

---

1 The Law Reform Commission is a statutory body the functions of which are to keep the law under review and to formulate proposals for its reform.

Table 16.1 gives statistics relating to applications for barring and protection orders, which are the most widely used remedy in cases involving domestic violence.

Table 16.1

	1992	1993	1994	1-8-94 to 31-7-95
Applications for Barring Orders made to District Court	4,321	4,318	4,457	4,448
Applications for Protection Orders made to District Court	2,772	2,706	3,091	3,107

Legal Aid

The Scheme of Civil Legal Aid and Advice was introduced on a non-statutory basis in 1980. Under the Scheme, the services of lawyers are made available to persons at little or no cost, subject to a means test. The Government, conscious of the need to make extra resources available to the Legal Aid Board to enable it to improve the level of service it can provide to needy applicants, increased the amounts of funds available to the Board from the Exchequer from £1.568m in 1989 to £3.006m for 1993, to £4,972m in 1994, £6.2m in 1995 and £6.5m in 1996. The Civil Legal Aid Act, 1995 put the Scheme on a statutory basis and a board (the Legal Aid Board) to operate the Scheme was established with effect from 11 October, 1996. Members of the Board are appointed by the Minister for Equality and Law Reform

Marriage Counselling

Where the parties agree, marriage counselling can be of immense value in cases of domestic disputes and there are excellent voluntary organisations who help couples in difficulty. The provision of assistance to such organisations by way of funding is one of the ways in which the State can address the issue of marriage breakdown including domestic violence. In 1994 and 1995 the Government provided £750,000 for marriage counselling agencies, which was an increase of 250% over that provided in 1993. The provision in 1996 is £900,000 and the scheme has been extended to include grants for counselling of children. A particular aim of the increased funding was to enable the organisations involved in marriage counselling to expand and develop their services.

Women and Child Unit

In 1993 a new Women and Child Unit was established in Dublin by the Garda Commissioner to deal specifically with complaints of domestic violence. This unit is staffed by Gardaí who are highly trained and experienced in dealing with domestic violence and sexual assaults. It's functions include:

- Overseeing the investigation of offences of domestic violence, child sexual abuse and other violent and sexual offences committed against women and children in the Dublin Metropolitan Area. Enforcement practices in respect of protection and barring orders are also included.
- Liaising with organisations, both statutory and voluntary, which deal with violent or sexual crime against women and children, and drafting a protocol on the role of Garda Síochána in these cases, and standard operating procedures for the investigation and enforcement of protection and barring orders.
- Developing a body of investigative skill which can be imparted through training programmes.

Refuges

Refuge or hostel facilities are available in each of the eight health boards and the level of financial support provided by the health boards to the refuges represents about 90% of the total expenditure on such services. Financial support has also been made available for counselling and telephone helpline services for victims of domestic violence.

The Minister for Health is fully committed to further development of appropriate services within the health area for victims of domestic violence. The Discussion Document – 'Developing a Policy for Women's Health' – identifies services for victims of domestic violence as one of the priorities for the further enhancement of services to protect women's health.

The Department of Health provided support to a project to develop a protocol on the identification, treatment and referral of women presenting at hospital casualty departments who are victims of domestic violence. This protocol is now being applied in the accident and emergency departments in hospitals in the Eastern Health Board area.

Working Group on Violence Against Women

The Office of the Tánaiste has been assigned responsibility, at central Government level, for co-ordinating action to deal with the problem of violence against women. It has established a Working Group to develop a co-ordinated response and strategy on mental, physical or sexual violence against women – with a particular focus on domestic violence. The Group will:

- examine existing services and supports (emergency, interim and long-term) for women who have been subjected to violence;
- examine legislation dealing with the victims and perpetrators of domestic violence;
- make recommendations on how legislation, services and supports could be improved and made more effective.

The Group will also examine the causes of violence against women (including, if necessary, initiating research) and make recommendations for a comprehensive preventative strategy as well as looking at rehabilitation programmes for perpetrators of such crimes.

Membership of the Working Group is drawn from relevant Government Departments and State agencies. It also includes individuals, experts and practitioners from relevant service delivery areas. The Group is chaired by Eithne Fitzgerald, TD, Minister of State at the Office of the Tánaiste. The Group had its first meeting on 15 October, 1996 and has been asked to report to Government by the end of February, 1997.

Individual Government Departments and agencies will continue to be responsible for the actual development and delivery of services for women who have been the victims of violence.

Other Legislative Developments

The Criminal Law (Rape) (Amendment) Act, 1990 represents a significant improvement in the legal protection afforded to victims of sexual assaults and is a statement of the seriousness with which these crimes are viewed by the Government and the legislature. It also abolished certain rules which were regarded as being offensive to women. The main provisions of the Act are:

- abolition of the rule that a husband cannot generally be found guilty of raping his wife,
- creation of two new offences of aggravated sexual assault and rape under Section 4 (to cater for offences involving sexual penetration which do not come within the traditional definition of rape), each with a maximum penalty of life imprisonment;
- extension of the special evidential and anonymity provisions (which previously only applied to rape victims) to all sexual assault victims.

This Act also provides for trials of rape and aggravated sexual assault to be held in the Central Criminal Court with the public but not the media being excluded. During the trial anonymity is afforded the complainant and plaintiff.

The Criminal Evidence Act, 1992 makes it easier for witnesses to give evidence in criminal cases involving physical or sexual abuse, by providing that in such cases witnesses' evidence may be given by live television link.

The Criminal Justice Act, 1993 enables unduly lenient sentences to be appealed and places an obligation on courts, when determining sentences for sexual and violent offences, to take into account the effect on the victim. It also empowers the court to order a convicted person to pay compensation to the victim.

The Criminal Law (Incest Proceedings) Act, 1995 provides that while members of the public shall be excluded from incest proceedings the press shall be entitled to attend and to report on such proceedings subject to a requirement that no information must be published which would enable an alleged incest victim to be identified. In addition, the Act increased to life imprisonment the maximum penalty to which a person convicted of incest can be sentenced.

In 1992 a total of 127 cases of rape were reported but in only 63 instances were criminal proceedings commenced. In the same year 300 cases of indecent assault on females were reported with 160 cases being brought for criminal proceedings. See also commentary under Article 12.

Investigation of Child Sexual Abuse Cases

The procedures to be followed by the health boards in the investigation of child sexual abuse are set out in the **Child Abuse Guidelines** issued by the Department of Health in 1987. These guidelines were amended in 1995 by the **Guidelines for the Notification of Suspected Cases of Child Abuse between Health Boards and Gardaí** in relation to the circumstances in which the Health Boards and the Gardaí are to notify suspected cases of child abuse to each other and in relation to the consultations that should take place between both agencies following a notification.

In February, 1996 the Department of Health issued a discussion document on mandatory reporting entitled **Putting Children First** as a basis for widespread consultations with various interest groups. This document sets out the main arguments for and against the introduction of a new mandatory reporting law which would place designated professionals under a legal obligation to report known or suspected cases of child abuse to the relevant authorities. As part of the consultative process interested bodies and individuals were invited to make submissions on the issues raised in the document.

The consultation process culminated in a consultative forum on **The Reporting of Child Abuse – The Contribution of Mandatory Reporting** in September, 1996.

Over two hundred submissions from groups and individuals were received in response to Putting Children First. Every person or group who made a submission was invited to this Forum. The submissions reflected the wide diversity of views on mandatory reporting and this divergence of opinion was also in evidence at the consultative forum.

The Minister of State for Health carefully considered the views expressed at the forum and in January, 1997 circulated **Putting Children First – Promoting and Protecting the Rights of Children**. He announced his decision not to introduce mandatory reporting in the immediate future. However, the Minister of State detailed a series of initiatives arising from views expressed during the consultative process which will further promote the rights of children and protect their welfare. The Minister has given a commitment that the initiatives will be reviewed after three years to assess the effectiveness of their impact on the reporting arrangements for suspected cases of child abuse.

1(a) The same right to enter marriage

Another unspecified personal right which is latent in Article 40 of the Constitution is the right to marry. (Ryan v Attorney General, 1965 Irish Reports 294) This right is also implied by Article 41.3.1 which specifically commits the State to guarding

> *with special care the institution of Marriage, on which the Family is founded, and to protect it against attack.*

The Constitutional Review Group (see Part I, paragraph 2.1), while favouring an express pledge by the State to protect marriage, did not favour the retention of the words "upon which the family is founded" in Article 41.3.1°. It was felt that these words have led to an exclusively marriage based definition of the family, which no longer accords fully with the social structure in Ireland. It proposed a revised Article 41 to include, inter alia, the following elements:

- a right for all persons to marry in accordance with the requirements of the law, and to found a family;
- a pledge by the State to protect the family based on marriage in its Constitution and authority;
- a guarantee to all individuals of respect for their family life, whether based on marriage or not.

1(b) ***The same right freely to choose a spouse and to enter into marriage only with their free and full consent.***

Marriage itself is not defined by the Irish Constitution. However, common law defines marriage as the "voluntary union for life of one man and one woman to the exclusion of all others". In common law, a marriage is void if there is absence of consent.

1(c) ***the same rights and responsibilities during marriage and at its dissolution.***

The rights and responsibilities of spouses towards each other and of parents towards their children derive primarily from Articles 40 to 42 of the Constitution but are further regulated by statute law.

The Judicial Separation and Family Law Reform Act, 1989 abolished the action for divorce a mensa et thoro and replaced it with a new action for judicial separation. This can be obtained on wider grounds with substantially improved provision for dependent spouses and children. A spouse may now apply for a judicial separation on any one or more of the grounds that:

- the other spouse has committed adultery;
- the other spouse has behaved in such a way that the applicant cannot reasonably be expected to live with the other spouse;
- there has been desertion by the other spouse for a continuous period of one year immediately preceding the date of the application for a decree. Desertion includes conduct on the part of the other spouse that resulted in the applicant, with just cause, leaving and living apart from the other spouse;
- the spouses have lived separately for a continuous period of at least one year immediately preceding the date of the application where the other spouse consents to a decree being granted;
- the spouses have lived separately for a continuous period of three years immediate preceding the date of the application;
- the marriage has broken down to the extent that a normal marital relationship has not existed between the spouses for a period of at least one year immediately preceding the date of the application.

Prior to the 1989 Act the powers of the court in divorce a mensa et thoro proceedings to make orders in support of a spouse or dependent children were very limited. Under the 1989 Act the court was given wide powers to order financial relief: it was empowered (a) to order maintenance, as well as secured maintenance, which involves tying up capital assets so that they continue to be available for paying the maintenance ordered by the court; (b) to order lump sums; (c) to order the transfer of property, including the family home, between the spouses and to dependent children or to order that a spouse may occupy the family home for life. The court was also empowered to order the sale of property whenever it makes an order involving capital assets (e.g. a lump sum, transfer of property or a secured periodical payments order). The court was required to exercise its powers to make financial provision and property orders in a manner which shall seek to ensure that such provision is made for any spouse and dependent children as is adequate and reasonable having regard to all the circumstances. In making such orders the court was required to have regard to such matters as the income, earning capacity, property and other financial resources of the spouses and a spouse's contribution in caring for the family and looking after the family home.

While a judicial separation decree has the effect that it is no longer obligatory for the spouses to cohabit it does not legally end the marriage and, accordingly, does not permit remarriage.

The Family Law Act, 1995 repealed and re-enacted with amendments provisions in the 1989 Act on the powers of the court to deal with the financial consequences of a judicial separation and extended those powers to cases where a foreign decree of divorce or separation is entitled to recognition in the State. In addition the Act introduced a new type of order called a financial compensation order under which the court has power to assign a life assurance policy in favour of a spouse and dependent children and an order called a pension adjustment order under which the court in separation proceedings can assign an interest in an occupational pension to a spouse and dependent children.

The Act empowers the courts for the first time to make appropriate financial provision for the protection and support of persons with close connections with Ireland whose marriage has been dissolved abroad and the decree of divorce is entitled to recognition in Ireland.

Under the *Domicile and Recognition of Foreign Divorces Act, 1986* Irish law will recognise a divorce granted in a foreign jurisdiction if either of the parties was domiciled in that jurisdiction at the time of the institution of the divorce proceedings. When a divorce is granted in a country other than a country where either of the spouses is domiciled, the divorce will be recognised under Irish law if it is recognised by the law of the country where both spouses are domiciled, or if they are domiciled in different countries, if it is recognised by the laws of both those countries. Where the divorce is granted in England and Wales, Scotland, Northern Ireland, the Channel Islands or the Isle of Man it will be recognised in Ireland if either spouse is domiciled in any of these jurisdictions whether or not this is the jurisdiction in which the divorce is granted.

In 1992 the Government published a White Paper entitled **Marital Breakdown – A Review and Proposed Changes**. The Paper reflected the outcome of a comprehensive review by a number of Government Departments of developments in family law since 1986 and specified the need for further changes. The Paper contained options for an amendment of the Constitution to remove the constitutional ban on divorce and a commitment by the Government to the holding of a referendum on the question of its removal.

A referendum on divorce was held on 24 November, 1995. The referendum was carried by a small majority. The proposal in the referendum was that Article 41.3.2^0 which states as follows:

> *2° No law shall be enacted providing for the grant of a dissolution of marriage.*

should be deleted and replaced with the following:

> *2° A court designated by law may grant a dissolution of marriage, where, but only where, it is satisfied that:*
>
> *(i) at the date of the institution of the proceedings, the spouses have lived apart from one another for a period of, or periods amounting to, at least four years during the previous five years;*
>
> *(ii) there is no reasonable prospect of a reconciliation between the spouses;*
>
> *(iii) such provision as the court considers proper having regard to the circumstances exists or will be made for the spouses, any children of either or both of them and any other person prescribed by law, and*
>
> *(iv) any further conditions prescribed by law are complied with.*

The referendum result was upheld in a challenge to it in the High Court. The decision of the High Court was upheld on 12 June, 1996 on appeal before the Supreme Court.

The Family Law (Divorce) Act, 1996 containing powers similar to those in the Family Law Act, 1995 for separation proceedings to deal with the financial consequences of divorce was enacted on 27 November, 1996 and comes into operation on 27 February, 1997.

Legal Aid/Counselling/Mediation

In response to the problems of marriage breakdown substantial funding is provided by the Government for legal aid, counselling and mediation.

An extensive scheme of legal aid is provided on a wide geographical basis. Grants are paid under a new Government scheme to a number of voluntary organisations providing marriage guidance and counselling services. See commentary on Legal Aid, above.

The Family Mediation Service established in 1986 on a pilot basis is now permanent. The Scheme provides a service to assist a husband and wife whose marriage has broken down to reach a voluntary agreement (without the need for a court to become involved) about issues such as arrangements for children, property, the family home, maintenance and succession rights. There is a development plan in place for the Service since 1994.

1(d) ***the same rights and responsibilities as parents, irrespective of their marital status, in matters relating to their children; in all cases the interests of the children shall be paramount;***

1(f) ***the same rights and responsibilities with regard to guardianship, wardship, trusteeship and adoption of children, or similar institutions where these concepts exist in national legislation; in all cases the interests of the children shall be paramount.***

Article 42.5 of the Constitution recognises the

> *natural and imprescriptible rights of the child.*

On acceding to this Convention, Ireland entered the following reservation in relation to Article 16.1 (d) and (f):

> Ireland is of the view that the attainment in Ireland of the objectives of the Convention does not necessitate the extension to men of rights identical to those accorded by law to women in respect of the guardianship, adoption and custody of children born out of wedlock and reserves the right to implement the Convention subject to that understanding.

Arising from a Supreme Court decision (The State (Nicolaou) v An Bord Uchtála (the Adoption Board)) a natural father is considered not to have any constitutionally protected rights to his child.

Under the *Guardianship of Infants Act, 1964*, a court, in deciding any question relating to the custody, guardianship or upbringing of a child, must regard the welfare of the child as the first and paramount consideration.

The 1964 Act provides that the father and mother of a child born within marriage shall be joint guardians of the child and that the mother of a child born outside marriage shall be the guardian of that child. Section 12 of the *Status of Children Act, 1987* amended the Guardianship of Infants Act, 1964 to provide that

> where the father and mother of an infant have not married each other the court may, on the application of the father, by order appoint him to be a guardian of the infant.

There is a simple court procedure where there is agreement between the father and mother.

Arising from a finding by the European Court of Human Rights, Ireland is now obliged to give natural fathers to whom children are born in the context of 'family life', as interpreted by the European Court of Human Rights, a legal opportunity to establish a relationship with that child (Keegan v Ireland (1994) 18EHRR 342).

The Constitutional Review Group considered this issue. The Group recognised that there has been much criticism of the continued constitutional ostracism of natural fathers. The

Group felt that this can be readily understood in relation to those natural fathers who either live in a stable relationship with the natural mother, or have established a relationship with the child. However, it concluded that there does not appear to be justification for giving constitutional rights to every natural father simply by reason of biological links and thus include fatherhood resulting from rape, incest or sperm donorship.

The Review Group considered that the solution appears to lie in following the approach of Article 8 of the European Convention on Human Rights in guaranteeing to every person respect for 'family life' which has been interpreted to include non-marital family life but yet requiring the existence of family ties between the mother and the father. This may be a way of granting constitutional rights to those fathers who have, or had, a stable relationship with the mother prior to birth, or subsequent to birth with the child, while excluding persons from such rights who are only biological fathers without any such relationship. In the context of the Irish Constitution it would have to be made clear that the reference to family life included family life not based on marriage.

A child may be made a ward of court and any important action in relation to the child can only be taken with the consent of the court. The concept of "trusteeship" of children is not known under Irish law.

A Bill to update the law on certain aspects of guardianship is being drafted.

Legal adoption is permanent and is for the benefit of children. The welfare of the child is the first and paramount consideration. The present law permits the adoption of orphans and children born outside marriage, including, in certain circumstances, children whose natural parents subsequently marry each other. In addition, in exceptional cases, the High Court may authorise the adoption of children whose parents have failed in their duty towards them. Children born within marriage may be adopted under this provision.

Legislation governs the eligibility of persons to adopt. Normally, applicants must be a married couple who are living together or the mother or father or a relative of the child (relationship to a child born outside marriage is traced through the mother only) or a widow or a widower. An adoption order in favour of a single or separated person may be made in exceptional cases where it is desirable in the interests of the child.

The Adoption Board (an independent statutory body) cannot make an adoption order unless it is satisfied that each of the adopting parents is a suitable person to have parental rights and duties in respect of the child.

The consent of every person who is a parent or guardian of the child or has charge of or control over, the child is normally required. As most adoptable children are born outside marriage, the consent of the natural mother only is normally required.

The consent of the natural father is required where:

(a) he marries the natural mother after the birth of the child, or

(b) he is appointed a guardian of the child or is granted custody of the child pursuant to a court order or otherwise.

New adoption legislation providing for a new statutory procedure for consulting the fathers of children born outside marriage being proposed for adoption is currently before Dáil Éireann (the Irish House of Representatives). The need for this legislation arises from a ruling by the European Court of Human Rights in a case brought against the Irish Government by the father of a child born outside marriage, who was adopted against the father's wishes. (Keegan v Ireland (1994)).

1(e) The same rights to decide freely and responsibly on the number and spacing of their children and to have access to the information, education and means to enable them to exercise these rights.

The right of men and women to decide freely and responsibly on the number and spacing of their children is enshrined in Irish law.

Under the guidelines issued to health boards by the Department of Health on the development of comprehensive family planning services in March, 1995, the following must be provided:

- education, counselling and advice on all legal methods of contraception;
- natural methods of family planning;
- medical contraceptives, such as the pill and spermicides;
- non-medical contraceptives, such as condoms, IUDs and diaphragms;
- male and female sterilisation services i.e. vasectomies and tubal ligations.

These must be accessible and available on an equitable basis.

In addition, the General Medical Services Scheme, which provides free medical care for persons on low incomes, has been extended to include, in addition to the contraceptive pill, the following services without charge for eligible women:

- intra uterine contraceptive devices;
- contraceptive caps;
- contraceptive diaphragms;
- spermicidal contraceptives and lubricating jelly where used in association with contraceptive devices.

See also Commentary under Article 12.

1(g) The same personal rights as husband and wife, including the right to choose a family name, a profession and an occupation.

Upon marriage, both spouses may retain their name and the family name may be the name of either spouse or a combination of both names. Irish marriage laws do not require a woman to take the name of her husband on marriage.

Men and women have equal rights to choose a profession and an occupation. These rights are guaranteed in the Constitution.

1(h) The same rights for both spouses in respect of the ownership, acquisition, management, administration, enjoyment and disposition of property, whether free of charge or for a valuable consideration

Under Section 2 of the Married Women's Status Act, 1957 a married woman is in the same position as a single woman and as her husband in so far as acquiring and disposing of property is concerned. There is no system of community property in Ireland.

As regards the ownership of the family home, where a wife contributes by money to the purchase of the property by her husband in his sole name or contributes either directly or indirectly towards the repayment of mortgage instalments (an indirect payment could be a contribution to the general family fund) she will, in the absence of an agreement or an arrangement to the contrary, be entitled to a share in the beneficial interest of that property proportionate to her contribution.

However, where a husband makes a contribution to the purchase of property in his wife's sole name there is a rebuttable presumption that he intended to make an advance in favour of his wife. He will have no claim to a beneficial share in the property unless that presumption is rebutted. Similarly, where a husband contributed either directly or indirectly to the repayment of mortgage charges on property which is in the legal ownership of his wife there will a presumption of advancement and only in the event of a rebuttal of that presumption will the husband have a claim to a beneficial share of the property.

An attempt was made in 1993 to enact legislation designed to give both spouses equal rights of ownership in the matrimonial home and household effects (the Matrimonial Home Bill, 1993). However, the Bill did not become law as the Supreme Court found it to be repugnant to the provisions of Article 41 of the Constitution which concern the family. Consideration is being given to alternative ways whereby joint ownership of the family home might be encouraged.

Under section 25 of the Housing Act, 1988 new house grants which were normally payable only in the case of first time own occupiers may also be payable where a previous owner-occupier is acquiring a new house following marital breakdown.

2. ***The betrothal and the marriage of a child shall have no legal effect, and all necessary action, including legislation, shall be taken to specify a minimum age for marriage and to make the registration of marriages in an official registry compulsory.***

Under Irish law a marriage is void unless there is the consent of both partners. The Family Law Act, 1995 increased the minimum age for marriage to eighteen years and removed the need for parental consent to the marriage of persons under twenty-one years of age. The Act also provides, subject to conditions, for three months notice to be given of marriage.

Under the Registration of Marriages (Ireland) Act, 1863, the official registration of marriage is obligatory.

Appendix 1

Convention on the Elimination of All Forms of Discrimination against Women

The States Parties to the present Convention,

Noting that the Charter of the United Nations reaffirms faith in fundamental human rights, in the dignity and worth of the human person and in the equal rights of men and women,

Noting that the Universal Declaration of Human Rights affirms the principle of the inadmissibility of discrimination and proclaims that all human beings are born free and equal in dignity and rights and that everyone is entitled to all the rights and freedoms set forth therein, without distinction of any kind, including distinction based on sex,

Noting that the States Parties to the International Covenants on Human Rights have the obligation to ensure the equal right of men and women to enjoy all economic, social, cultural, civil and political rights,

Considering the international conventions concluded under the auspices of the United Nations and the specialised agencies promoting equality of rights of men and women,

Noting also the resolutions, declarations and recommendations adopted by the United Nations and the specialized agencies promoting equality of rights of men and women,

Concerned, however, that despite these various instruments extensive discrimination against women continues to exist,

Recalling that discrimination against women violates the principles of equality of rights and respect of human dignity, is an obstacle to the participation of women, on equal terms with men, in the political, social, economic and cultural life of their countries, hampers the growth of the prosperity of society and the family and makes more difficult the full development of the potentialities of women in the service of their countries and of humanity,

Concerned that in situations of poverty women have the least access to food, health, education, training and opportunities for employment and other needs,

Convinced that the establishment of the new international economic order based on equity and justice will contribute significantly towards the promotion of equality between men and women,

Emphasizing that the eradication of *apartheid*, of all forms of racism, racial discrimination, colonialism, neo-colonialism, aggression, foreign occupation and domination and interference in the internal affairs of States is essential to the full enjoyment of the rights of men and women,

Affirming that the strengthening of international peace and security, relaxation of international tension, mutual co-operation among all States irrespective of their social and economic systems, general and complete disarmament, and in particular nuclear disarmament under strict and effective international control, the affirmation of the principles of justice, equality and mutual benefit in relations among countries and the realization of the right of peoples under alien and colonial domination and foreign occupation to self-determination and independence, as well as respect for national sovereignty and territorial integrity, will promote social progress and development and as a consequence will contribute to the attainment of full equality between men and women,

Convinced that the full and complete development of a country, the welfare of the world and the cause of peace require the maximum participation of women on equal terms with men in all fields,

Bearing in mind the great contribution of women to the welfare of the family and to the development of society, so far not fully recognized, the social significance of maternity and the role of both parents in the family and in the upbringing of children, and aware that the role of women in procreation should not be a basis for discrimination but that the upbringing of children requires a sharing of responsibility between men and women and society as a whole,

Aware that a change in the traditional role of men as well as the role of women in society and in the family is needed to achieve full equality between men and women,

Determined to implement the principles set forth in the Declaration on the Elimination of Discrimination against Women and, for that purpose, to adopt the measures required for the elimination of such discrimination in all its forms and manifestations,

Have agreed on the following:

PART I

Article 1

For the purposes of the present Convention, the term "discrimination against women" shall mean any distinction, exclusion or restriction made on the basis of sex which has the effect or purpose of impairing or nullifying the recognition, enjoyment or exercise by women, irrespective of their marital status, on a basis of equality of men and women, of human rights and fundamental freedoms in the political, economic, social, cultural, civil or any other field.

Article 2

States Parties condemn discrimination against women in all its forms, agree to pursue by all appropriate means and without delay a policy of eliminating discrimination against women and, to this end, undertake:

(*a*) To embody the principle of the equality of men and women in their national constitutions or other appropriate legislation if not yet incorporated therein and to ensure, through law and other appropriate means, the principal realization of this principle;

(*b*) To adopt appropriate legislative and other measures, including sanctions where appropriate, prohibiting all discrimination against women;

(*c*) To establish legal protection of the rights of women on an equal basis with men and to ensure through competent national tribunals and other public institutions the effective protection of women against any act of discrimination;

(*d*) To refrain from engaging in any act or practice of discrimination against women and to ensure that public authorities and institutions shall act in conformity with this obligation;

(*e*) To take all appropriate measures to eliminate discrimination against women by any person, organization or enterprise;

(*f*) To take all appropriate measures, including legislation, to modify or abolish existing laws, regulations, customs and practices which constitute discrimination against women;

(*g*) To repeal all national penal provisions which constitute discrimination against women.

Article 3

States Parties shall take in all fields, in particular in the political, social, economic and cultural fields, all appropriate measures, including legislation, to ensure the full development and advancement of women, for the purpose of guaranteeing them the exercise and enjoyment of human rights and fundamental freedoms on a basis of equality with men.

Article 4

1. Adoption by States Parties of temporary special measures aimed at accelerating *de facto* equality between men and women shall not be considered discrimination as defined in the present Convention, but shall in no way entail as a consequence the maintenance of unequal or separate standards; these measures shall be discontinued when the objectives of equality of opportunity and treatment have been achieved.

2. Adoption by States Parties of special measures, including those measures contained in the present Convention, aimed at protecting maternity shall not be considered discriminatory.

Article 5

States Parties shall take all appropriate measures:

(*a*) To modify the social and cultural patterns of conduct of men and women, with a view to achieving the elimination of prejudices and customary and all other practices which are based on the idea of the inferiority or the superiority of either of the sexes or on stereotyped roles for men and women;

(*b*) To ensure that family education includes a proper understanding of maternity as a social function and the recognition of the common responsibility of men and women in the upbringing and development of their children, it being understood that the interest of the children is the primordial consideration in all cases.

Article 6
States Parties shall take all appropriate measures, including legislation, to suppress all forms of traffic in women and exploitation of prostitution of women.

PART II

Article 7
States Parties shall take all appropriate measures to eliminate discrimination against women in the political and public life of the country and, in particular, shall ensure to women, on equal terms with men, the right:

(*a*) To vote in all elections and public referenda and to be eligible for election to all publicly elected bodies;

(*b*) To participate in the formulation of government policy and the implementation thereof and to hold public office and perform all public functions at all levels of government;

(*c*) To participate in non-governmental organisations and associations concerned with the public and political life of the country.

Article 8
States Parties shall take all appropriate measures to ensure to women, on equal terms with men and without any discrimination, the opportunity to represent their Governments at the international level and to participate in the work of international organizations.

Article 9

1. States Parties shall grant women equal rights with men to acquire, change or retain their nationality. They shall ensure in particular that neither marriage to an alien nor change of nationality by the husband during marriage shall automatically change the nationality of the wife, render her stateless or force upon her the nationality of the husband.

2. States Parties shall grant women equal rights with men with respect of the nationality of their children.

PART III

Article 10

States Parties shall take all appropriate measures to eliminate discrimination against women in order to ensure to them equal rights with men in the field of education and in particular to ensure, on a basis of equality of men and women:

(*a*) The same conditions for career and vocational guidance, for access to studies and for the achievement of diplomas in educational establishments of all categories in rural as well as in urban areas; this equality shall be ensured in pre-school, general, technical, professional and higher technical education, as well as in all types of vocational training;

(*b*) Access to the same curricula, the same examinations, teaching staff with qualifications of the same standard and school premises and equipment of the same quality;

(*c*) The elimination of any stereotyped concept of the roles of men and women at all levels and in all forms of education by encouraging coeducation and other types of education which will help to achieve this aim and, in particular, by the revision of textbooks and school programmes and the adaptation of teaching methods;

(*d*) The same opportunities to benefit from scholarships and other study grants;

(*e*) The same opportunities for access to programmes of continuing education, including adult and functional literacy programmes, particularly those aimed at reducing, at the earliest possible time, any gap in education existing between men and women;

(*f*) The reduction of female student drop-out rates and the organization of programmes for girls and women who have left school prematurely;

(*g*) The same opportunities to participate actively in sports and physical education;

(*h*) Access to specific educational information to help to ensure the health and well-bring of families, including information and advice on family planning.

Article 11

1. States Parties shall take all appropriate measures to eliminate discrimination against women in the field of employment in order to ensure, on a basis of equality of men and women, the same rights, in particular:

    (*a*) The right to work as an inalienable right of all human beings;

    (*b*) The right to the same employment opportunities, including the application of the same criteria for selection in matters of employment;

    (*c*) The right to free choice of profession and employment, the right to promotion, job security and all benefits and conditions of service and the right to receive vocational training and retraining, including apprenticeships, advanced vocational training and recurrent training;

(*d*) The right to equal remuneration, including benefits, and to equal treatment in respect of work of equal value, as well as equality of treatment in the evaluation of the quality of work;

(*e*) The right to social security, particularly in cases of retirement, unemployment, sickness, invalidity and old age and other incapacity to work, as well as the right to paid leave;

(*f*) The right to protection of health and to safety in working conditions, including the safeguarding of the function of reproduction.

2. In order to prevent discrimination against women on the grounds of marriage or maternity and to ensure their effective right to work, States Parties shall take appropriate measures:

(*a*) To prohibit, subject to the imposition of sanctions, dismissal on the grounds of pregnancy or of maternity leave and discrimination in dismissals on the basis of marital status;

(*b*) To introduce maternity leave with pay or with comparable social benefits without loss of former employment, seniority or social allowances;

(*c*) To encourage the provision of the necessary supporting social services to enable parents to combine family obligations with work responsibilities and participation in public life, in particular through promoting the establishment and development of a network of child-care facilities;

(*d*) To provide special protection to women during pregnancy in types of work proved to be harmful to them.

3. Protective legislation relating to matters covered in this article shall be reviewed periodically in the light of scientific and technological knowledge and shall be revised, repealed or extended as necessary.

Article 12

1. States Parties shall take all appropriate measures to eliminate discrimination against women in the field of health care in order to ensure, on a basis of equality of men and women, access to health care services, including those related to family planning.

2. Notwithstanding the provisions of paragraph 1 of this article, States Parties shall ensure to women appropriate services in connection with pregnancy, confinement and the postnatal period, granting free services where necessary, as well as adequate nutrition during pregnancy and lactation.

Article 13

States Parties shall take all appropriate measures to eliminate discrimination against women in other areas of economic and social life in order to ensure, on a basis of equality of men and women, the same rights, in particular:

(*a*) The right to family benefits;

(*b*) The right to bank loans, mortgages and other forms of financial credit;

(*c*) The right to participate in recreational activities, sports and all aspects of cultural life.

Article 14

1. States Parties shall take into account the particular problems faced by rural women and the significant roles which rural women play in the economic survival of their families, including their work in the non-monetized sectors of the economy, and shall take all appropriate measures to ensure the application of the provisions of this Convention to women in rural areas.

2. States Parties shall take all appropriate measures to eliminate discrimination against women in rural areas in order to ensure, on a basis of equality of men and women, that they participate in and benefit from rural development and, in particular, shall ensure to such women the right:

   (*a*) To participate in the elaboration and implementation of development planning at all levels;

   (*b*) To have access to adequate health care facilities, including information, counselling and services in family planning;

   (*c*) To benefit directly from social security programmes;

   (*d*) To obtain all types of training and education, formal and non-formal, including that relating to functional literacy, as well as, *inter alia*, the benefit of all community and extension services, in order to increase their technical proficiency;

   (*e*) To organize self-help groups and co-operatives in order to obtain equal access to economic opportunities through employment or self-employment;

   (*f*) To participate in all community activities;

   (*g*) To have access to agricultural credit and loans, marketing facilities, appropriate technology and equal treatment in land and agrarian reform as well as in land resettlement schemes;

   (*h*) To enjoy adequate living conditions, particularly in relation to housing, sanitation, electricity and water supply, transport and communications.

PART IV

Article 15

1. States Parties shall accord to women equality with men before the law.

2. States Parties shall accord to women, in civil matters, a legal capacity identical to that of men and the same opportunities to exercise that capacity. In particular, they shall give women equal rights to conclude contracts and to administer property and shall treat them equally in all stages of procedure in courts and tribunals.

3. States Parties agree that all contracts and all other private instruments of any kind with a legal effect which is directed at restricting the legal capacity of women shall be deemed null and void.

4. States Parties shall accord to men and women the same rights with regard to the law relating to the movement of persons and the freedom to choose their residence and domicile.

Article 16

1. States Parties shall take all appropriate measures to eliminate discrimination against women in all matters relating to marriage and family relations and in particular shall ensure, on a basis of equality of men and women:

   (*a*) The same right to enter into marriage;

   (*b*) The same right freely to choose a spouse and to enter into marriage only with their free and full consent;

   (*c*) The same rights and responsibilities during marriage and at its dissolution;

   (*d*) The same rights and responsibilities as parents, irrespective of their marital status, in matters relating to their children; in all cases the interests of the children shall be paramount;

   (*e*) The same rights to decide freely and responsibly on the number and spacing of their children and to have access to the information, education and means to enable them to exercise these rights;

   (*f*) The same rights and responsibilities with regard to guardianship, wardship, trusteeship and adoption of children, or similar institutions where these concepts exist in national legislation; in all cases the interests of the children shall be paramount;

   (*g*) The same personal rights as husband and wife, including the right to choose a family name, a profession and an occupation;

   (*h*) The same rights for both spouses in respect of the ownership, acquisition, management, administration, enjoyment and disposition of property, whether free of charge or for a valuable consideration.

2. The betrothal and the marriage of a child shall have no legal effect, and all necessary action, including legislation, shall be taken to specify a minimum age for marriage and to make the registration of marriages in an official registry compulsory.

PART V

Article 17

1. For the purpose of considering the progress made in the implementation of the present Convention, there shall be established a Committee on the Elimination of Discrimination against Women (hereinafter referred to as the Committee) consisting, at the time of entry into force of the Convention, of eighteen and, after ratification of or accession to the Convention by the thirty-fifty State Party, of twenty-three experts of high moral standing and competence in the field covered by the Convention. The experts shall be elected by States Parties from among their nationals and shall serve in their personal capacity, consideration being given to equitable geographical distribution and to the representation of the different forms of civilization as well as the principal legal systems.

2. The members of the Committee shall be elected by secret ballot from a list of persons nominated by States Parties. Each State Party may nominate one person from among its own nationals.

3. The initial election shall be held six months after the date of the entry into force of the present Convention. At least three months before the date of each election the Secretary-General of the United Nations shall address a letter to the States Parties inviting them to submit their nominations within two months. The Secretary-General shall prepare a list in alphabetical order of all persons thus nominated, indicating the States Parties which have nominated them, and shall submit it to the States Parties.

4. Elections of the members of the Committee shall be held at a meeting of States Parties convened by the Secretary-General at United National Headquarters. At that meeting, for which two thirds of the States Parties shall constitute a quorum, the persons elected to the Committee shall be those nominees who obtain the largest number of votes and an absolute majority of the votes of the representatives of States Parties present and voting.

5. The members of the Committee shall be elected for a term of four years. However, the terms of nine of the members elected at the first election shall expire at the end of two years; immediately after the first election the names of these nine members shall be chosen by lot by the Chairman of the Committee.

6. The election of the five additional members of the Committee shall be held in accordance with the provisions of paragraphs 2, 3 and 4 of this article, following the thirty-fifty ratification or accession. The terms of two of the additional members elected on this occasion shall expire at the end of two years, the names of these two members having been chosen by lot by the Chairman of the Committee.

7. For the filling of casual vacancies, the State Party whose expert has ceased to function as a member of the Committee shall appoint another expert from among its nationals, subject to the approval of the Committee.

8. The members of the Committee shall, with the approval of the General Assembly, receive emoluments from United Nations resources on such terms and conditions as the Assembly may decide, having regard to the importance of the Committee's responsibilities.

9. The Secretary-General of the United Nations shall provide the necessary staff and facilities for the effective performance of the functions of the Committee under the present Convention.

Article 18

1. States Parties undertake to submit to the Secretary-General of the United Nations, for consideration by the Committee, a report on the legislative, judicial, administrative or other measures which they have adopted to give effect to the provisions of the present Convention and on the progress made in this respect:

   (*a*) Within one year after the entry into force for the State concerned; and

   (*b*) Thereafter at least every four years and further whenever the Committee so requests.

2. Reports may indicate factors and difficulties affecting the degree of fulfilment of obligations under the present Convention.

Article 19

1. The Committee shall adopt its own rules of procedure.

2. The Committee shall elect its officers for a term of two years.

Article 20

1. The Committee shall normally meet for a period of not more than two weeks annually in order to consider the reports submitted in accordance with article 18 of the present Convention.

2. The meetings of the Committee shall normally be held at United Nations Headquarters or at any other convenient place as determined by the Committee.

Article 21

1. The Committee shall, through the Economic and Social Council, report annually to the General Assembly of the United Nations on its activities and may make suggestions and general recommendations based on the examination of reports and information received from the States Parties. Such suggestions and general recommendations shall be included in the report of the Committee together with comments, if any, from States Parties.

2. The Secretary-General shall transmit the reports of the Committee to the Commission on the Status of Women for its information.

Article 22

The specialized agencies shall be entitled to be represented at the consideration of the implementation of such provisions of the present Convention as fall within the scope of their activities. The Committee may invite the specialized agencies to submit reports on the implementation of the Convention in areas falling within the scope of their activities.

PART VI

Article 23

Nothing in this Convention shall affect any provisions that are more conducive to the achievement of equality between men and women which may be contained:

(*a*) In the legislation of a State Party; or

(*b*) In any other international convention, treaty or agreement in force for that State.

Article 24

States Parties undertake to adopt all necessary measures at the national level aimed at achieving the full realization of the rights recognized in the present Convention.

Article 25

1. The present Convention shall be open for signature by all States.

2. The Secretary-General of the United Nations is designated as the depository of the present Convention.

3. The present Convention is subject to ratification. Instruments of ratification shall be deposited with the Secretary-General of the United Nations.

4. The present Convention shall be open to accession by all States. Accession shall be effected by the deposit of an instrument of accession with the Secretary-General of the United Nations.

Article 26

1. A request for the revision of the present Convention may be made at any time by any State Party by means of a notification in writing addressed to the Secretary-General of the United Nations.

2. The General Assembly of the United Nations shall decide upon the steps, in any, to be taken in respect of such a request.

Article 27

1. The present Convention shall enter into force on the thirtieth day after the date of deposit with the Secretary-General of the United Nations of the twentieth instrument of ratification or accession.

2. For each State ratifying the present Convention or acceding to it after the deposit of the twentieth instrument of ratification or accession, the Convention shall enter into force on the thirtieth day after the date of the deposit of its own instrument of ratification or accession.

Article 28

1. The Secretary-General of the United Nations shall receive and circulate to all States the text of reservations made by States at the time of ratification or accession.

2. A reservation incompatible with the object and purpose of the present Convention shall not be permitted.

3. Reservations may be withdrawn at any time by notification to this effect addressed to the Secretary-General of the United Nations, who shall then inform all States thereof. Such notification shall take effect on the date on which it is received.

Article 29

1. Any dispute between two or more States Parties concerning the interpretation or application of the present Convention which is not settled by negotiation shall, at the request of one of them, be submitted to arbitration. If within six months from the date of the request for arbitration the parties are unable to agree on the organization of the arbitration, any one of those parties may refer the dispute to the International Court of Justice by request in conformity with the Statute of the Court.

2. Each State Party may at the time of signature or ratification of this Convention or accession thereto declare that it does not consider itself bound by paragraph 1 of this article. The other States Parties shall not be bound by that paragraph with respect to any State Party which has made such a reservation.

3. Any State Party which has made a reservation in accordance with paragraph 2 of this article may at any time withdraw that reservation by notification to the Secretary-General of the United Nations.

Article 30

The present Convention, the Arabic, Chinese, English, French, Russian and Spanish texts of which are equally authentic, shall be deposited with the Secretary-General of the United Nations.

IN WITNESS WHEREOF the undersigned, duly authorized, have signed the present Convention.

Appendix 2

Text of remaining Irish Government Reservations to the Convention

Article 13(b) and (c)

The question of supplementing the guarantee of equality contained in the Irish Constitution with special legislation governing access to financial credit and other services and recreational activities, where these are provided by private persons, organisations or enterprises is under consideration. For the time being Ireland reserves the right to regard its existing law and measures in this area as appropriate for the attainment in Ireland of the objectives of the Convention.

Article 15

With regard to paragraph 3 of this Article, Ireland reserves the right not to supplement the existing provisions in Irish law which accord women a legal capacity identical to that of men with further legislation governing the validity of any contract or other private instrument freely entered into by a woman.

Articles 16, 1(d) and (f)

Ireland is of the view that the attainment in Ireland of the objectives of the Convention does not necessitate the extension to men of rights identical to those accorded by law to women in respect of the guardianship, adoption and custody of children born out of wedlock and reserves the right to implement the Convention subject to that understanding.

Articles 11(1) and 13(a)

Ireland reserves the right to regard the Anti-Discrimination (Pay) Act, 1974 and the Employment Equality Act, 1977 and other measures taken in implementation of the European Economic Community standards concerning employment opportunities and pay as sufficient implementation of Articles 11, 1(b), (c) and (d).

Ireland reserves the right for the time being to maintain provisions of Irish legislation in the area of social security which are more favourable to women than men.